P9-CRA-747

Ellen Raskin

Twayne's United States Authors Series
Children's Literature

Ruth K. MacDonald, Editor

TUSAS 579

Ellen Raskin.
Photo by David Gahr.

Ellen Raskin

Marilynn Strasser Olson
Southwest Texas State University

Twayne Publishers • Boston
A Division of G. K. Hall & Co.

MIDDLEBURY COLLEGE LIBRARY

Ellen Raskin
Marilynn Strasser Olson

Copyright 1991 by G. K. Hall & Co.
All rights reserved.
Published by Twayne Publishers
A division of G. K. Hall & Co.
70 Lincoln Street
Boston, Massachusetts 02111

Copyediting supervised by Barbara Sutton.
Book production by Janet Z. Reynolds.
Typeset by Compset, Inc., Beverly, Massachusetts.

10 9 8 7 6 5 4 3 2 1

The paper used in this publication meets the minimum requirements
of American National Standard for Information Sciences—Permanence
of Paper for Printed Library Materials, ANSI Z39.48-1984. ∞™

Printed and bound in the United States of America.

Library of Congress Cataloging-in-Publication Data

Olson, Marilynn Strasser
    Ellen Raskin / Marilynn Strasser Olson.
        p.   cm. — (Twayne's United States authors series ; TUSAS
    579. Children's literature)
    Includes bibliographical references and index.
    ISBN 0-8057-7627-3
    1. Raskin, Ellen—Criticism and interpretation.   2. Children's
stories, American—History and criticism.   I. Title.   II. Series:
Twayne's United States authors series ; TUSAS 579.   III. Series:
Twayne's United States authors series.   Children's literature.
PS3568.A696Z8   1991
813'.54—dc20   90-27121

Contents

Preface

I remember the evening I first read *the tattooed potato & other clues* in a farmhouse bedroom in Geneseo, New York, soon after its publication. I read it three times, marveling at my discovery. I felt a strong urge to hang garlands on the doorknob of the author, though I did not know then that her doorknob was really not very far away and her house was in the book itself.

Years later, I suppose this is my garland, though, as Johnson remarked in his letter to Chesterfield, too late. I have had to weigh and sift Raskin's books more than most of the people I encounter who say, "She's the best," when her name is mentioned, but I know what they mean.

Trained as an artist and first achieving success as a free-lance illustrator, Raskin won many prizes for her thousand book jackets, her illustrations for more than 30 books for children and young adults, and for 12 picture books of her own. Though the Raskin picture books have a characteristically witty and sophisticated style, the canon, which I discuss in this book, is remarkably varied and shows interesting links in attitude and subject matter to her later writing. Her versatility was demonstrated again when, in the 1970s, she produced four unusual novels called "puzzle-mysteries." These novels entered mainstream children's fiction when the last published work, *The Westing Game*, won the Newbery Medal and lasting popularity among its readers.

Although Raskin's work was regularly and favorably reviewed in her lifetime, little scholarship is available on her picture books or novels. Because she wrote and spoke about her books (especially as they related to her childhood memories), the tapes, interviews, and videos collected at the University of Wisconsin

Cooperative Children's Book Center in Madison were an important source of information about her life and work. As a Notable Wisconsin Author (named by the Wisconsin Library Association) and University of Wisconsin alumnus, Raskin had many ties to the center. Raskin's family gave her illustrations and other materials relating to her work to the Kerlan Collection at the University of Minnesota; we used these for reproduction in this book.

Because Raskin always made her family and background appear essential to her inspiration and because the role of the background was a puzzle, it was important to talk to Raskin's husband, Dennis Flanagan; her daughter, Susan Metcalfe; her sister, Lila Fink; and her editor at Dutton, Ann Durell, to try to understand these connections. (I am indebted to their intelligence and kindness.) People who heard her speeches and witnessed her library visits, while not individually noted here, have also helped. David Gahr, the photographer whose portrait of Raskin appears in this book, knew her first as a friend in Wisconsin.

Innovation, talent, and critical success are enough to explain Raskin's importance to her chosen field. Her comic vision, her investigation of the American dream, and her original plots deserve attention as part of the fields of American literature and American humor, as well.

Jane Austen said of Mr. Bennet that . . . "where other powers of entertainment are wanting, the true philosopher will derive benefit from such as are given." Raskin said that her art training had sharpened her perception of what was "out of drawing," incongruous, and disproportionate in life. Naturally, this forms the basis of much of her humor. But Raskin, a "true philosopher" in her books, also sought beauty: "The visual artist looks and can see beauty in the absurd, magic in the mundane." Games as arbiters of rules and objectives are a metaphor for a vision of life that can be ordered, understood, and won. Raskin's admirers are likely to be those who recognize the limits of daily living and admire the vision and fancy footwork that it takes to achieve perspective and grace.

Acknowledgments

The illustrations in the books are from original artwork donated by Raskin's family to the Kerlan Library at the University of Minnesota. Tapes of speeches, workshops, interviews, and radio shows cited are preserved in the Cooperative Children's Book Center, University of Wisconsin, Madison, which also holds the manuscript materials of *The Westing Game* and a collection of Raskin's printed works. Although the responsibility for the views expressed in this work is mine, I owe thanks to Dennis Flanagan, Ann Durell, Lila Fink, and Susan Metcalfe for interviews about Raskin's life and work; Theresa Bayer, Kristina Faber Irot, and Kathi Jensen for consultation; and Molly Nelson Haber, Dennis Flanagan, Don Olson, Ruth Stevenson, and Steve Wilson for reading and advising me about the manuscript.

Chronology

1928   Ellen Raskin born 13 March in Milwaukee, Wisconsin, oldest child of Sol and Margaret (Goldfisch) Raskin.

1935   Family leaves to find work in California. Returns eight months later.

1945–1948   Attends University of Wisconsin, majoring in journalism during freshman year, thereafter in fine arts.

1948   Leaves Wisconsin for New York City. Gives birth to a daughter, Susan. Works for advertising agency to learn trade.

1955   Begins career as a free-lance illustrator. Completes her first jacket illustration, for *Satan in Goray* by Isaac Bashevis Singer. Raskin eventually illustrated more than 1,000 jackets.

1956   Illustrates Claire H. Bishop's *Happy Christmas*.

1959   Illustrates and prints Dylan Thomas's *Child's Christmas in Wales* as a sample to show publishers that she can illustrate books. New Directions publishes the popular edition, launching Raskin's successful career as an illustrator.

1960   Jean Karl, editor at Atheneum, having seen the *Child's Christmas in Wales* woodcuts, suggests that Raskin illustrate Ruth Krauss's manuscript for *Mama, I Wish I Was Snow; Child, You'd Be Very Cold*.

1962   Illustrates (woodcut) Krauss's *Mama, I Wish I Was Snow; Child, You'd Be Very Cold*.

1964   Illustrates *This is 4: The Idea of a Number* by Arthur Razzell and Kenneth Watts, which is soon followed by two others in the series: *Probability: The Science of Chance* and *A Question of Accuracy.*

1965   Illustrates (pointillism) *Poems of Edgar Allan Poe,* selected by Dwight MacDonald.

1966   After three brief, unsuccessful marriages, marries Dennis Flanagan, editor of *Scientific American,* on 17 October. Illustrates (woodcut) Louis Untermeyer's *Paths of Poetry.* Illustrates (woodcut) and writes musical accompaniments for William Blake's *Songs of Innocence,* which is included in the American Institute of Graphic Arts Best Books Exhibit. Illustrates (woodcut) Molly Cone's *The Jewish Sabbath.* Writes and illustrates her first picture book, *Nothing Ever Happens on My Block* which wins a *New York Herald Tribune* Children's Book Week Award and is named *New York Times* Choice of Best Illustrated Children's Books of the Year.

1967   Illustrates (pen and ink) *D. H. Lawrence: Poems Selected for Young People,* edited by William Cole. Illustrates (mixed media) *Ellen Grae* by Vera and Bill Cleaver. Writes and illustrates *Silly Songs and Sad,* a book of verse with dramatically contrasting illustrations.

1968   Illustrates (reproducing period illustration) *Books: A Book to Begin On* by Susan Bartlett. Writes and illustrates *Spectacles,* which is named *New York Times* Choice of the Best Illustrated Children's Books of the Year and is an American Library Association Notable Children's Book. Illustrates *Lady Ellen Grae* by Vera and Bill Cleaver. Illustrates (pen and ink) *Piping Down the Valleys Wild: Poetry for the Young of All Ages,* edited by Nancy Larrick. Illustrates (woodcut) *Inatuk's Friend* by Suzanne Stark

Morrow. Illustrates (mixed media) *A Paper Zoo,* a book of modern verse edited for children by R. K. Weiss. Illustrates (pen and ink) *We Alcotts* by Aileen Fisher and Olive Rabe. Illustrates two more books in the mathematics series: *Symmetry* and *Circles and Curves* by Arthur G. Razzell and Kenneth George Oliver Watts.

1969 Writes and illustrates *Ghost in a Four-Room Apartment.* Illustrates *Come Along!* by Rebecca Caudill. Illustrates *Shrieks at Midnight: Macabre Poems, Eerie and Humorous,* edited by Sara and John Brewton. Illustrates the last of the mathematics series, *Three and the Shape of Three,* by Arthur G. Razzell and Kenneth George Oliver Watts.

1970 Writes and illustrates *A & The: or, William T. C. Baumgarten Comes to Town.* Illustrates and adapts Christina Rossetti's *Goblin Market.*

1971 Writes and illustrates first long novel, *The Mysterious Disappearance of Leon (I Mean Noel),* edited by Ann Durell, which is an ALA Notable Children's Book. Writes and illustrates *The World's Greatest Freak Show.*

1972 Writes and illustrates *Franklin Stein. The Mysterious Disappearance of Leon (I Mean Noel)* is included in the Children's Book Showcase.

1973 Writes and illustrates *Moe Q. McGlutch, He Smoked Too Much.* Writes and illustrates *Who, Said Sue, Said Whoo?,* which is included in the AIGA Best Books Exhibit and is an ALA Notable Children's Book.

1974 Writes and illustrates second long novel, *Figgs & phantoms,* which is included in the AIGA Best Books Exhibit and is an ALA Notable Children's Book. *Who, Said Sue, Said Whoo?* is included in the Children's Book Showcase. Writes and illustrates third long novel, *the tattooed potato & other clues*. Writes and illustrates *Moose, Goose & Little Nobody*.

1975 *Figgs & phantoms* is named Newbery Honor Book and is included in the Children's Book Showcase. *the tattooed potato & other clues* is an ALA Notable Children's Book.

1976 Writes and illustrates *Twenty-Two, Twenty-Three,* which is an ALA Notable Children's Book. *the tattooed potato & other clues* receives Mystery Writers of America Edgar Allan Poe Special Award.

1978 Writes her last published long novel, *The Westing Game,* which wins a *Boston Globe/Horn Book* Fiction Award and is an ALA Notable Children's Book.

1979 *The Westing Game* receives Newbery Medal.

1981 Named Notable Wisconsin Author by the Literary Awards Committee of the Wisconsin Library Association.

1984 Dies 8 August in New York City.

1

Biographical Sketch

> It is the book that is the important thing, not who I am or how I did it, but the book. Not me, the book. I fear for the book in this age of inflated personalities, in which the public's appetite for an insight into the lives of the famous has been whetted by publicity-puffers and profit-pushers into an insatiable hunger for gossip. I worry that who-the-writer-is has become of more interest than what-the-writer-writes. I am concerned that this dangerous distortion may twist its way into children's literature. . . . It is the book that lives, not the author. It is not I that is being honored here tonight; it is my book.
>
> —Newbery Medal Acceptance, Dallas, Texas,
> 26 June 1979

In light of Ellen Raskin's stern comments about the book, not the author, being important and the bitter comments in *the tattooed potato* about the "ogling crowd,"[1] it is hard to feel that writing about Raskin the woman is a good idea. Certainly, nothing that one can write is apt to be what she herself wanted to hear.

But Ellen Raskin always talked about her books as being about her family and her life, particularly her life as a child in Wisconsin: "Strange as my books are, they're really autobiographical."[2] She was the most personal of authors, assuring us in her speeches, essays, and interviews that her characters—even the background figure pouring water out of the window on the postman in *Nothing Ever Happens on My Block*—were people she had known. She had great appeal as a speaker. People at the libraries she visited remember her vividly and lovingly because she was unconventional and unpretentious. The glimpses she gave into her family history were tough and funny. What is more apt to make people think that they need to know more?

The things that we know but that she did not say are part of the reason. It was certainly unsettling to people who had not known her intimately to learn from Alice Bach's *Horn Book* tribute[3] or from her death notices that she had been seriously ill. She had, in fact, been charming, bright, and ceaselessly industrious while she had a painful connective tissue disorder and a high fever, a condition that had been troublesome at intervals and increasingly hard to endure. She was slightly more open about this near the end of her life, but for the most part it was a secret, and not the sort of secret that most other people would consider keeping, or, indeed, *could* have kept.

Raskin often said that her heroines resembled her. They are, as a group, unusually reserved. For example, Mona, Raskin's favorite heroine in *Figgs & phantoms,* does not tell her cousin Fido (or anyone else) about Uncle Flo's afterlife. The reason for keeping the secret is not obvious in the story, though it is consistent with Mona's earlier behavior. And Dickory in *the tattooed potato* doesn't tell her brother Donald that she has been nearly killed by the men who murdered their parents. In *The Westing Game,* Turtle doesn't tell her husband, Theo, that Westing is alive, despite their happy marriage. Raskin's own life and death are mysterious for similar reasons. More than other people, she liked a mystery and had motivations that were not readily accessible to others.

The public Ellen Raskin, though, was a wonderful person. The picture of Raskin that emerges from her husband's essay "The Raskin Conglomerate"[4] is a rich one. It tells us about her thousand book jackets, her extensive career as a free-lance illustrator, her musical talent that we glimpse in the musical settings she composed and illustrated for Blake's *Songs of Innocence,* her remarkable stock market expertise, and her exuberant ability to fill the rest of her impossibly busy life with garden vegetables, lovely food, games, art, sports enthusiasms, zoos, tap-dancing, pets, and her family. Flanagan's portrait of Raskin shows her "invincible originality"("CP"), energy, and talent.

The Wisconsin childhood that Raskin personally shared with her public combined racy tales of her mother's family, "the funny ones,"[5] with Depression era poverty and personal misery. "Those were hard times, the Depression years," she said; "they made me a humorist. Just about anything is funny after that" ("Characters," 620). We find from these autobiographical portraits that Raskin was an excellent student, ahead of herself in school, short in the midst of "Nordic" giants,[6] and myopic. She played the piano (until it was repossessed) and wanted to be a pianist. Her loneliness, which had the positive effect of sending her to books, was exacerbated by anti-Semitism and frequent moves ("six or seven before sixth grade" ["CP"]) but also seems to have been concerned with simply not finding other people with her tastes and ambitions.

Raskin's own speeches and essays also tell about her dear stepgrandfather Hersh, a pious Orthodox Jew who was the model for Uncle Flo in *Figgs & phantoms*. Grandfather Hersh's photograph resembles Augie Kunkel in *The Mysterious Disappearance of Leon (I Mean Noel)* as well. Her step-grandfather died when Raskin was 10. The essays also describe her younger sister, Lila, now an English professor, who acted in her childhood plays and whose personality seemed to Raskin to come out in many of her characters (one of them Turtle). Raskin's essays are also about her mother, who married young, and her mother's family, models for Sister and the Figgs, and her good-natured, irresponsible father, Sol, who died just before her daughter was born. Sol Raskin became Newt Newton in *Figgs & phantoms* and Jake Wexler in *The Westing Game* ("Characters," 625). Finally, the speeches tell about a childhood in which, whatever its other shortcomings, she had time to read and "follow [her] own pursuits" (Hinchcliffe interview). Like some other creative people, Raskin retained an unusual nearness to her formative years and the ability to draw on early impressions and feelings in her work. "I remember almost everything that happened to me as a child,"[7] she said.

But no one remembers a childhood objectively. In Raskin's case, it appears that her view of it may have been different from the view that other people in her position might have had. Undoubtedly, to some extent it was created and reworked as she reworked her stories. On the copy of *The Westing Game* that she gave her sister, she wrote, with reference to the two main characters of the story, "To Turtle from the Bomber."[8] Although she felt closest to *Figgs & phantoms,* the family arrangement in *The Westing Game*—two sisters, one neglected, one smothered—appears to have been modeled on the childhood that she and her sister shared and agreed about. A beautiful, musical child, Raskin appears to have been especially loved by her parents and her mother's extended family connection, whereas her sister, who was asthmatic and often ill, was not given either the attention or the overprotectiveness that went with it. Raskin's reaction to this situation seems to have been like Angela (the Bomber) Wexler's in *The Westing Game;* she told her sister that she envied her her role as neglected child and longed to have the freedom and ability to control her own life that came when she went away to college.

The poverty that obsessed her all her life was not continual or long lasting. Her father lost his drug store in the Depression and could not initially establish a new life in California because he lacked the appropriate license. It is this anxious interlude that Raskin mentioned most; it made a horrifyingly strong impression on her, one that did not leave her even when she was a prosperous and financially secure adult. Although the Depression made a difference in her family life, Raskin had nice clothes, a piano, and favorable expectations by the time she entered high school, where she was active and popular.

Notably, Raskin's desire to create, to escape, to do the best she could in her chosen profession was much stronger than her fear of poverty or loneliness. When she left college and went to New York City, she spent several years there learning the practical applications of her art, sharing Chinese dinners with her young daughter, marrying briefly and collecting unemployment, which renewed her acquaintance with financial struggling. But this time, Raskin was in control of her own life. After illustrating and then printing Dylan Thomas's *A Child's Christmas in Wales* on her own press to show to art directors, she achieved steady employment as a free-lance illustrator remarkably quickly.

Because of Raskin's sensitive treatment of discrimination in her books, her own position as a Jewish child in pre–World War II Milwaukee is of interest. Raskin's younger sister, Lila Fink, remembers the "No Jews Allowed" signs that they witnessed at a lakeside resort (and tore up, nightly, from a boat) and being stoned by Catholics on Yom Kippur (and throwing the stones back). But Lila herself remembers their high school, which included boys and girls of varying ethnicity, better than isolation or prejudice.

The loneliness Raskin described and partly attributed to being the only Jewish child in her class is evidently from the same early period as her painful memories of poverty: the time of the many moves that her family made before sixth grade and that her sister was too young to remember as clearly. These years coincided with the most active years of the German-American Bund and similar attempts to establish Hitler's national socialism in the German-American community. No doubt this accounts for the perhaps isolated, but horrifying, "no Jews or dogs" mentality. Clearly, Raskin was strongly influenced by things that happened to her during her elementary school days at a time when she was first developing a sense of her own social identity. As an adult, Raskin strongly identified with outsiders and had strong sympathy with victims of discrimination.

In a speech at Milwaukee in 1979, Raskin said that from the age of 10 she wanted to be famous. She described this desire through one of her outrageous stories about a visitor with bedbugs who attracted considerable family notoriety for this affliction. This was certainly a story that her audience could not have expected as they met to honor *Westing Game* with a Banta Award and celebratory button. But it is an interesting declaration that seems important to Raskin's life and work.

Raskin elaborated on this theme in the radio interviews in 1979 and 1981 because as a Notable Wisconsin Author she was in a position of having to explain why she left Wisconsin. Fame in illustrations meant going to New York City, she explained, the only place where she felt she could get to the top of her profession. The size and impersonality of New York City also explains why fame, to Raskin, apparently was compatible with extreme reserve. Indeed, the two seemed to go together in her mind. "I wanted to go to a large city where I would be anonymous and no one would know what a dumb kid I had been." "Somehow I would have to leave Wisconsin to go to a place where it was possible to be famous" (Hinchcliffe interview). This is explained in the Banta Speech by her declaration that what she had learned from the eccentric visitor with bedbugs was "that fame was not the person you are but what you did."[9] This is not the usual definition of fame, and it is difficult to decide how much fame means simply the freedom to create and live the creative life, and how much it meant the rewards that might come with it.

As she said in her speech "Me and Blake, Blake and Me" at Simmons College,[10] Raskin was "famous for a year" when she won the 1979 Newbery Medal, although she had been celebrated as an author/illustrator long before. Both Alice Bach, and Raskin herself commented upon Raskin's unusual admission that she was actively trying to get the Caldecott and Newbery prizes (Bach, 164).[11] This frankness about ambition, the sort of thing some people would never admit, attests to her continuing desire and need for tangible proof that she was successful.

The frankness seems to mean, though, more that she had done her homework than she had hubris about her own work. That is, she had studied the other prize winners and knew what was considered valuable in a book. She had looked at the creative process in writers that she liked as well as writers she disliked, in order to determine where she fell or wanted to fall. She told hopeful writers that they could tell a great deal from bad books, for they could decide what to avoid and what had made a book fail. She also told them that they couldn't imitate. Raskin chose to be deliberate rather than haphazard about the work she did and to keep high standards and heroes before her.

In children's books, the Newbery and Caldecott prizes are deservedly valued, but Raskin's heroes were not all famous in their lives and had extraordinary, rather than accessible, talents: "Piero della Francesca, Velazquez, Milton, Franz Schubert, Henry James, Joseph Conrad" (Flanagan, 395), and Blake. If one activity admires and emulates genius, admitting that one wants the Newbery prize is more an interesting quirk than the admission of raw ambition. It is also notable that if Raskin had been intending to become famous in these terms, she might not have chosen illustration or children's books as her medium.

Prizes and awards, of which Raskin had many, are the kind of fame that help in making a living and provide a great deal of potential work to do, particularly for a successful illustrator who can also write her own picture book texts. After the birth of her daughter, Raskin worked to keep her daughter safe. She wanted to take care of her, but she wanted her daughter to know how to earn money too. At the age of 12, therefore, Susan Metcalfe started doing color separations for her mother for pay, and Raskin later got work for her with others as well.[12] Many Raskin books tell us the troubles that follow chasing money and success to the exclusion of family or values, but the Depression did not teach people to be indifferent to making a living.

Finally, Raskin chose to live in New York because a famous person in a big town can have a new persona, can have the opportunity and the forum to create a public image to go with the achievement. This is what those Raskin essays and speeches did. This is also, perhaps, another aspect of the kind of control that Raskin liked to have over her life and her work.

The Creative Process

Curiously, in Raskin's work, the creative process seems to have eluded her control. The author structured new worlds to live in when she started a novel, but the real world appears to have moved in while she was writing.

One of the aspects of how she wrote a book that Raskin often explained was her use of a "swipe file." A swipe file is a collection of pictures cut out of magazines and other sources that illustrators use as models: teenagers sitting, children standing, lions sleeping. Raskin went to her swipe file to choose her characters. When describing *the tattooed potato,* for example, she explained how the choice of topic entered into the choice of characters: It was to be about art, so there would be an artist; it was a children's book, so there ought to be a young character; it was a mystery, so there would be criminals; and, presumably because she had an appropriate address in Greenwich Village, it would be in her own house ("CP"). Going to a swipe file meant that before she started she knew what each of these necessary people and the floorplan of their house looked like. They had a certain structure and personal characteristics already.

Because Raskin was a visual artist, knowing what the people and place looked like before she started was important. But it is a process that sounds like an elaborate parlor game with more than usual artificiality. The naming process in *Figgs & phantoms,* for example, appears to have started with the descriptions of figs in an encyclopedia.

If there are going to be personal elements in writing that starts from this kind of structuring, they are going to sneak in during the writing. They are not planned at the outset. For example, the picture of Turtle Wexler from the swipe file was collected from a Sunday supplement article on the wonders of orthodontic surgery. This article showed how proper surgical techniques could construct a chin for patients with receding chins and realign mouths to give more attractive facial contours. Turtle was the "before" picture, her receding chin an integral part of her creation (and one that was never turned into an "after"!). Raskin's sister did not visually resemble the picture of Turtle any more than Raskin looked like the vapid, flowery file picture of Angela. Indeed, since she said that it was much easier to do a picture book because it was not confrontational for her (Roginski, 171), one can imagine that Raskin might have had no conscious desire to get herself or her loved ones into autobiography at all, although she enjoyed what had happened to her life and loved ones afterward. She said that she had written several drafts of *The Westing Game* before she realized that Westing had fooled her, too: that the corpse was alive.

Susan Metcalfe, Raskin's daughter, read the drafts of Raskin's longer manuscripts first; Ann Durell, her editor, after. Raskin said that she could handle criticism best on her early drafts.[13] Some of the criticisms can be seen in little stick-on notes on her manuscripts to *The Westing Game,* which are housed at the Children's Cooperative Book Center at the University of Wisconsin. Durell remembers Raskin running up and down the aisle from the smoking section on an airplane (Raskin smoked, Durell didn't) asking, "What do you think?" "What are you writing there?" while she was trying to read and edit.[14] Though she was clearly very sensitive to criticism, Raskin said that she took about half of the critical suggestions. She argued half and conceded that half were perfectly just.

Raskin tried to be punctilious about accuracy in her novels because she felt that she owed it to the children. They needed to be able to trust her. She had that respect for them. If she mentioned judges or fireworks, she wanted to have the facts right. Ginny Moore Kruse, the Director of the Cooperative Children's Book Center and Raskin's personal friend, helped her with some of the Wisconsin references. Whether because of this accuracy, or only the honest spirit behind it, Raskin certainly did find people to trust her. In an interview with Dick Hinchcliffe of WHA radio in 1979, Raskin talked a little about the young people who wrote her letters, especially about the novels. "All," she said, "think they are weird and I am weird and we all understand each other" (Hinchcliff interview).

Raskin's novels and picture books tell us repeatedly that the way to deal with real life is to control it through the use of the imagination and through work that you love. Apparently, when her illness and pain finally caused her to fear that she would not be able to continue to do this, she took her own life. She left behind an uncompleted manuscript, a mystery novel without an ending.

"I Always Think of Water as Lake Michigan"

I think that anyone would be hard-pressed to explain the qualities that make someone distinctively midwestern, especially in
the case of a person who made so spectacular a transition to living
in New York City and who had some good reasons for finding her
hometown an uncomfortable place to be raised. In this case, when
Raskin had longed for freedom and to leave her home, it is interesting to see her later attachment to the Midwest. But surely no
one can quarrel with the satisfaction of going home again on one's
own terms.

Raskin's video interview, "The Creative Process of Ellen Raskin," shows her surrounded by her editors, family, friends, and
readers, a tribute to her personal and professional success in
adulthood. It also shows her affectionately touring Milwaukee,
pointing out the places she knew from the Raskin side of the family: her step-grandfather's house, the four-room apartment,
Mount Sinai Hospital where her father worked as a pharmacist.
If these places and people have been transformed by humor, by
determination, by writing, so be it. The book's the thing.

2

Illustrations for Others

I want them to be surprises.
(Roginski, 168)

When Ellen Raskin left the University of Wisconsin for New York City to establish her career and support herself and her young daughter by commercial art, she had hurriedly to switch from a fine arts background to producing salable material. She worked for an advertising agency, doing paste-up work and in time producing a number of memorable advertising illustrations.

In Raskin's file boxes of original work at the Kerlan Library, *Satan in Goray* by Isaac Bashevis Singer (1955) was noted as being her first book jacket. Although it is difficult to reconstruct the history of the more than 1,000 book jackets that she made during her years as a free-lance illustrator and designer of books, 100 are at the Kerlan Library at the University of Minnesota, and more are available at the Children's Book Center at the University of Wisconsin at Madison.

Raskin made all kinds of jackets for many kinds of books: mysteries, novels, children's books, and religious treatises. A substantial number in the collection are for academic and otherwise-serious works: *Gypsy Ballads of García Lorca, Errand into the Wilderness,* the Kittredge Shakespeare. Many of the jackets would be familiar to the generation that went to college in the mid-sixties because textbooks of poetry, history, American thought, sociology, and philosophy often are found with her jackets or covers.

Perhaps of special note to the Raskin admirer aware of her passion for social justice is the remarkably sinister cover for Gustavus Myers's *History of Bigotry in the United States* and, in a different way, the cheerful cover for Leland Gralapp's *Boom!*, which includes a palm tree made out of dollars and is reminiscent of Mona's palm in *Figgs & phantoms* and Otis Amber and the cover for *The Westing Game*. Children's literature scholars will remember the work for Madeline L'Engle's novels, including the original cover for *A Wrinkle in Time*.

Dennis Flanagan, Raskin's husband, pointed out in "The Raskin Conglomerate," that at one per week it would take 20 years to produce so many jackets. Raskin not only took less time, but she had a full career as an author/illustrator as well. Illustrating in woodcuts (which have to be physically carved out for every cover), she experimented with techniques to shorten the process. She also simply had to work very hard.

Throughout her illustrating and writing careers, Raskin's work was marked by fastidiousness and respect for the art of making books. Books as objects were important to her; when she was writing novels, she adjusted the size of the printer's symbols she used to decorate the text and edited her text to fit the spaces, just as one might in a picture book. She thought of the reading experience as embracing the sensual experience of the feel of the cover (which is why she did not like library bindings) and the surprises and pleasures that could be put into the otherwise-empty copyright and beginning pages.

Although Raskin was an illustrator and designer of books before she ever considered writing them, in her novels the desire to paint and to create art starts with the printing process. In *the tattooed potato,* for example, Dickory's interest in painting begins when she first sees some art books in her parents' pawn shop. The most characteristic process for a puzzled Raskin heroine is to look things up, to find a reference. It is not surprising to know that Raskin loved to read, that she read the books she illustrated, and that she had a rare books collection.

Raskin's illustrations for other people in the children's literature field may be divided into four categories: decorated poetry books, decorated books that are not poetry books, illustrated and interpreted poetry books, and illustrated nonpoetry books. *Decorated,* a term she used to describe some of her own work, is used here to distinguish those pictures that have the least significance to the meaning of the book. The pictures make the book a more pleasant experience. They may set a mood or increase the reader's anticipation in opening the book, but they bear the least amount of burden of interpretation.

Raskin was fortunate in the books that she illustrated as a freelancer. Because many of the books she illustrated are books of lasting worth, her pictures will also last. It would be an exaggeration to say that everything she illustrated had a profound influence on her later writing or picture books, but a number give clues about the things she valued or ways she thought.

Decorated Books

Poetry

A Child's Christmas in Wales by Dylan Thomas was the book that Raskin first printed herself to show as a sample to publishers in an effort to become a free-lance illustrator, a project that set her on her way to success in the field. Like her academic texts, the textured paper, small size, and elegant printing of the 1959 volume evoke an era to many students of the 1960s and admirers of Dylan Thomas. Though the Christmas poem has been illustrated often, this was a memorable edition.

Raskin's woodcuts break the text gracefully on every other page. The light blue prints do not look like pictures of a real village in Wales; rather, they are pictures of a "village in one's youth"; the Christmas treats are "visions of sugarplums," not the specific items that Thomas received Christmas morning. The water and smoke—characteristically fluid and prominent in Raskin's later work—look elemental. In other words, Raskin created the dream side of the poem, which Thomas balances against the details of real cats and real aunts and real mufflers.

Poems of Edgar Allan Poe, edited by Dwight Macdonald (1965), is a collection of Poe poems and criticism divided into such categories as "the music of things" and "out of space and out of time." Raskin made a picture in the front of the book, and then two pictures (one under the heading on the title page of each section and another on the back of the title page opposite the first poem) for each section. The title page picture illustrates the title.

For example, "The Music of Things" is a black and white picture in pointillism of four gnarled trees with a wave at their roots and spirits entwining their branches. The reverse of this picture is a knight, "over the Mountains of the Moon" and "Down the valley of the Shadow," an accurate, text-linked illustration for "Eldorado." This pattern repeats for each section.

Raskin always read the material she was illustrating; here, she has set the mood for the book. The illustrations are romantic—not macabre but imaginative. The balance with the wide white margins is attractive. It is a handsome, readable book.

Paths of Poetry, edited by Louis Untermeyer (1966), is rather forbidding. Each poet whose work is featured in the book is represented in a biographical sketch by Untermeyer and a woodcut medallion in black and white (taken from the best-known likeness) by Raskin. The front page is a procession of these people in their typical dress marching to the left, drawing the eye to the right and the distance to make one turn the page. It has a pedagogical look, though the text is chosen to appeal to young people both by the brevity and aim of the biographies and the choice of poems. It looks solid, rather than accessible. Her illustrations include a portrait of Blake, which accompanies Untermeyer's biographical sketch of his early life and some of Blake's first, less anthologized, poems.

Piping Down the Valleys Wild, edited by Nancy Larrick (1968), is a good, lasting collection that has not been superseded. All of

Illustration from *Poems of Edgar Allan Poe.* © 1965 by Dwight Macdonald. Design by Ellen Raskin. Reproduced by permission of Harper & Row. Original artwork from the Kerlan Collection, University of Minnesota.

the poems have been tested for today's children and are drawn from many sources. It is appropriate to many age groups.

Like the decorations in *The Poems of Robert Herrick,* edited by Winfield Townley Scott (1967), the pictures are line drawings in black and white with a much lighter touch than the Untermeyer illustrations. The effect is to make both books simple and attractive in appearance. In Larrick's book, this seems appropriate: The sketches appear on the title pages of each section and are mostly bits of scenery or holiday-related items. The most imaginative is an illustration of Vachel Lindsey's poem about "the moon's the north wind's cookie."

In the Scott collection, the light, contemporary illustration seems to mirror the intention of the book but, initially, to be less appropriate to the poems themselves. *The Poems of Robert Her-*

rick is a volume of Herrick verse with modernized spelling and no explanatory notes or scholarly addendum. This volume, an attempt to make Herrick seem to be to the modern reader the charming poet that he was in his own day, is half-successful.

Raskin's decorations underscore the difficulty which is not of her making. For example, her serene line drawings of the sun and waves that accompany the text to Herrick's poem to Endymion Porter on his brother's death appropriately and helpfully pick up the images in the poem but are hard to reconcile with the baroque subject matter. It is not an easy poem, and to the reader (if not the writer) the death of Herrick's brother, although Herrick is comforted in his friendship with Endymion Porter, may seem the most notable part of it: "Sunk is my sight; set is my sun; And all the loom of life undone."

Although Raskin here appears to be carrying out the editor's desire for a classic and inviting tone, the poem seems to ask for something thornier and more anguished. It is likely, however, that the serenity of the drawings is in fact related to Raskin's work on *Goblin Market* and the very different *Songs of Innocence,* in which emotional distance from the subject matter seems integral to her interpretation. Here, with Herrick, a man of strong religious faith, the serene lightness of the drawings may be most appropriate: the indifference of nature to the poet's sorrow in the beginning; the ability of the poet to rise like the sun, renewed, at the end, may be more important than the metaphysical roads he takes to get to his quietus. Raskin's sensitive response to poetry and her own interest in renewal make it worth investigation, at any rate.

Shrieks at Midnight, edited by Sara and John Brewton (1969), uses a variation of the "cartoon" technique found in Raskin's own picture books. The faces are not so simple as in her own books, but have smiling mouths full of teeth that are undoubtedly meant to remind us of skulls and to make the pictures look satiric: "Macabre Poems, Eerie and Humorous." They use the flowing water and graceful lines familiar in Raskin picture books, which trivialize the tension in the text, while the stopped action of the fluid elements adds an itchy tension to the pictures.

As in the Herrick book, the decorations here distance us from the poems to ensure that they are "humorous" not "macabre." They serve the function that Thurber described when discussing his famous *New Yorker* cartoon of a fencer slicing the head off his opponent while shouting, "touché." Thurber's beheaded man could not possibly bleed and could clearly be reassembled without inconvenience or fuss; only under such conditions could that subject matter make a funny cartoon. In this volume, although a picture may be of a group chopping someone up to use him as turkey stuffing (the pictures decorate the section headings, which use an epigraph taken from the section), the nonnaturalistic drawing negate the morbid reality, while keeping the sarcastic tone.

Prose

Ellen Raskin did not illustrate her own novels, although she designed the text decorations and format. She did not feel that an illustrator should come between the reader and his or her own vision of the story. These books, therefore, show Raskin apparently working against the grain in order to fulfill her illustration contracts. The results are highly successful and remarkably varied.

The King of Men (1966), a prize-winning book by Olivia Coolidge, is a biography of Agaememnon. Like the Untermeyer poetry collection of the same year, Raskin's decorations here are in circles in black and white. These are highly successful, stylized Greek objects (ram's heads, ships) that resemble coins. The collection of a dozen coin-shapes appears on the title page and then individually adorns each chapter heading.

Ellen Grae (1967) and *Lady Ellen Grae* (1968) by Vera and Bill Cleaver are illustrated in a way that would interfere more with the imaginative process, in Raskin's theory, than the Greek decorations. Both, however, were given a less-than-realistic treatment, thus minimizing the illustrator's interference. The subject matter in each of these prize-winning books by the Cleavers is imaginative and unconventional. *Ellen Grae* is a realistic novel, but it concerns a fantastic and difficult situation. A young girl named Ellen Grae is told a horrible story by a retarded recluse, which could lead to his being institutionalized. The only reason that he is not is that, when Ellen finally has to tell the story to the authorities, she is not believed.

Although many incidents in the swamp setting might have been illustrated, Raskin dealt directly with the most important story line. The illustrations show Ellen Grae in a series of conversations in which the worrisome narrative is passed along (or evaded). The pictures aid the understanding of the novel: the picture showing the subject of the conversation appears above the people speaking. One can tell Ellen Grae's motives by her facial expressions. Since Ellen is often in trouble for lying, it is important to see her as a gifted storyteller (in the Huck Finn tradition) instead.

As Raskin would expect, her illustrations of Ellen Grae are less complex and interesting than the character in the text. However, the line drawings are clearly intended to relay the mood of the conversations rather than particular facial features; the visible "story" elements add to this nonrealistic effect. In fact, the Raskin drawings are unobtrusive and helpful.

Lady Ellen Grae appears to be a lighter book, although it has a serious core. This sequel deals with Ellen's transformation into a conventional, ladylike creature and her temporary removal from her swamp home. The illustrations, which show Ellen and her cousin, respectively, changing from swamp people to lady (and vice versa) in three steps, are humorous and appropriate. There is also a fine illustration, combining mood and image, in which a boat filled with Ellen, her friend, and her visiting relatives is in the center in a line drawing; a flying spoonbill and alligator, establishing the immutable setting, are shadowed in behind them.

We Dickinsons (1965) and *We Alcotts* (1968), by Aileen Fisher and Olive Rabe, respectively, are biographies of famous women seen through the eyes of another member of the family (Marmee Alcott, Austin Dickinson). These are personal, feminine-appearing books with symbolic decorations. Clearly, Raskin worked closely with the text, although her decorations form only the frontispiece and tiny chapter-heading decorations. In the Alcott book, the sisters and mother are line drawings filled in with calico patterns behind the enormous, important blank Bronson Alcott. Raskin used this technique again in her own novel, *The Mysterious Disappearance of Leon (I Mean Noel),* when she formed a similar contrast between Mrs. Carillon and other members of her family. The chapters are headed by charming little trees in full leaf or unleafed depending upon whether the mood of the chapter is happy or sad. Although this book is clearly not a major work for Raskin, her sensitivity in achieving the theme of the book in a single picture shows characteristic intelligence and ability.

The Emily Dickinson frontispiece is an image in pointillism of the Dickinson house (the floor plan is also included) with a large tree dominating the foreground. It conveys the outside borders of Emily Dickinson's adult world and the impingement of nature on that world.

Although Raskin did not want her illustrations for novels to intrude into the reading process, her skill and versatility are considerable and significantly improve the appearance and reinforce the intentions of the books discussed in this section.

Illustrated Books

Prose
Happy Christmas: Tales for Boys and Girls, edited by Claire Bishop (1956), contains the earliest available Raskin illustrations. The woodcuts are an important element in tying together this cheerful Christmas collection, one of three Raskin books printed for the Christmas market. The pictures have a primitive look: goblins locked inside a mountain are stacked to the top; needles grow directly out of the branches on the pine trees like teeth on a comb. The endpapers collect all the pictures from the inside of the book, antedating her later decision never to destroy the surprise of the pictures and her later tight control of composition. The sheep are less-finished versions of the ones used in the Coolidge book about Agaememnon, owing no doubt to Ras-

kin's youth and to the Christmas book's tone. Early interpretations of angels and pipers, both motifs used in the Blake work a decade later, are prominent in this book.

The Jewish Sabbath by Molly Cone (1966) is another holiday book with lasting values. Molly Cone interprets the Sabbath as freedom, and with that strong interpretation and the woodcut illustrations, it is a fine book for elementary children. The pictures most strongly resemble the cuts for Blake's *Songs of Innocence.* The symbols—candles, stars, bread, wine—take on a great solidity and serenity in the illustrations. The colors, like those of the Blake collection, are gold, green, and bluish green.

The Exploring Mathematics series by Arthur G. Razzell and K. G. O. Watts spanned the 1960s. These are sophisticated mathematics texts for fifth-graders done in one color and black. Although Asimov was annoyed by the red pages with black print in one of the books,[1] other reviewers unanimously appreciated the exciting look and pictorial interpretation at every opening.[2] The illustrations are vital in making the concept of symmetry, for example, accessible to the elementary student. Raskin does whole pages of rotating symbols for testing rotating symmetry and clarifies how such measurements as checking the gap on spark plugs are done. The books characteristically aid readers without patronising them.

Inatuk's Friend (1968) by Susan Stark Morrow is a beautiful picture book that could serve as a model of how to do front matter gracefully and enticingly. This story about the Arctic is done with stylized ice floes and a warm family, especially a tender sibling relationship. The colors (teal paper, gold skin, black hair, and black line) are arresting.

Books: A Book to Begin On (1968) by Susan Bartlett brings out Raskin's best because it deals with a topic so close to her own sensibility. The illustrations are integral to the message: Raskin's pictures, in gold and black on white pages, mix original work with her interpretations of Egyptian hieroglyphics, illuminated manuscripts, early type, and schoolbooks from the Colonial era. In her own picture book, *A & The; or, William T. C. Baumgarten Comes*

Illustration from *The Jewish Sabbath* by Molly Cone. © 1966. Illustrations © 1966 by Ellen Raskin. Reproduced by permission of Harper & Row. Original artwork from the Kerlan Collection, University of Minnesota.

to Town, Raskin similarly used the Bayeaux Tapestry in cartoon balloons to tell the story of William the Conqueror.

As in the later picture books, Raskin uses nonnaturalistic color here to emphasize the important part of a picture. She shows a sailing ship going to the New World in 1638, for example, in gold. The printing press—prominently located on the deck—is done in black. *Franklin Stein* (1972) used color in the same way. Franklin Stein's monster, Fred, is always in red, which similarly focuses the reader's attention.

Raskin was a traditional bookmaker. She was a rare book collector and lover of finely made books. *Books: A Book to Begin On,* with its wide, pleasing margins, garamond type, textured cover, and text about the story of bookmaking is a reminder of her standards and antecedents.

Poetry

Mama, I Wish I Was Snow; Child, You'd Be Very Cold (1962) is a wonderful book by Ruth Krauss inspired by the García Lorca poem "Canción Tonta." It consists of a set of poetically simple declarations by a child with his mother's responses: "Mama, I wish I was a skyscraper." "Child, how could I brush your hair?" The Raskin illustrations—bold prints in yellow, red, and black—are interesting for two reasons. First, they are essential to the understanding of the text. It takes an illustration to explain why a child who wishes he was "a fireplug" would then resemble "a child far away." In Raskin's picture, the bold red plug with yellow water does resemble the tiny black image of the child (with pompom hat and striped sweater) away over in the corner. Raskin thereby not only makes the idea feasible but, by the child's remote location, underscores the "how-could-mother-reach-you-and-hold-you" idea that is the theme of the interchange. She has responded imaginatively to the imaginative text.

Second, this "child as fireplug" or "child as skyscraper" idea is the characteristic signature of much of Raskin's work: Things are not as they seem. In both words and pictures, she offers surprises. The pictures of skyscrapers that can be deciphered by discovering that one of them is wearing basketball shoes, the child whose first

appearance is that of a fireplug, are imaginatively linked to the
Figg Newton Giant, the visions in *Spectacles,* Franklin Stein's
monster's appearance before and after the judging at the pet
show, and the one-word description of Isaac Bickerstaffe in *the
tattooed potato.* This book, which Jean Karl suggested Raskin un-
dertake at the beginning of her career as an illustrator, is a kind
of rosetta stone for Raskin's own texts.

Blake's *Songs of Innocence* (2 vols., 1966) is characteristic of
Raskin's work in another way. As she explained, Raskin under-
took the music and illustrations for *Songs* after she had made a
book jacket for *Improvisation in Music* by Gertrude Price Wollner
("Me and Blake," 348). Raskin read the book and decided to try
improvisation. Music was an important part of Raskin's early life;
as Flanagan explained (Flanagan, 394), music was Raskin's effort
to escape "imperfect reality" in her childhood, and she played the
piano very well.

Like Maurice Sendak, Raskin was passionate in her admiration
of Blake. Originally, there were musical settings for the *Songs of
Innocence.* Raskin improvised accompaniments to replace the lost
music and illustrated the poems with her own woodcuts because
some kind of Blakean reproduction would be too costly and im-
practicable ("Me and Blake," 348).

Raskin does for Blake's poems what she often does in her own
books. She isn't stinting the difficulties of the text, but she is
making it more accessible for the user. The songs are intended for
second-year piano or beginning guitar students. She suggests
how one could use the lines for duets; she leaves out the dynamics
so one can feel them individually. The Blake poems are, in fact,
easier as songs.

Raskin's woodcuts are timeless and mythological. The animals
and naked children are clearly in another world; expressions are
solemn, and the pictures are bold and straightforward in gold and
rust, bluish green and green. Lions, kings and angels coexist with
the children.

Raskin was aware of the evil in Blake's poems: the industrial
revolution, organized religion, child labor. She discusses evil and
Blake in her speech "Me and Blake, Blake and Me" presented at

the Simmons College Center for the study of Children's Literature ("Me and Blake," 351). She was conscious of Blake as an artist put out of work by the industrial revolution as well as an apprentice who became an adult with a skill that was being superseded. However, she illustrated not what she appears to have thought of as transient qualities in the poems but rather the innocent vision.

On the one hand, Raskin's interpretation is startling. For example, the poem about the chimney sweep is illustrated with the angel with a bright key and tiny, cheerful-looking sweeps with brushes forming a minor decoration. Yet the pathos of the poem and victimization of the narrator might seem to call for a more somber treatment: "My mother died when I was very young/My father sold me while yet my tongue/Could scarcely cry 'weep, 'weep, 'weep, 'weep." "On Another's Sorrow" ("Can a mother sit and hear / An infant groan an infant fear?") has a bird singing in a stylized tree with a posy of blossom at the top, its "grief & care" already forgotten.

Although the relation of pictures to poems in Blake's *Songs of Innocence,* mentioned, for example, by Jennifer Waller in her discussion of Maurice Sendak,[3] is itself absorbing, Raskin's interpretation of the *Songs* appears to be characteristic of more than her admiration for Blake and his style. To a great extent, Raskin separated what could be called "heart" and "head" in her work. The characters in her novels, for instance, solve puzzle-mysteries, often purely intellectual or creative exercises with clues that eventually add up to intellectual answers. The reasons for their doing so, however, depend on personal emotional problems that are not discussed directly. Solving the intellectual problems also provides solutions for the emotional problems by the end of the novel. But the "solutions" are not directly related to the emotional problems, nor do the characters directly admit to having any problems. The reader who does not have the capacity to perceive the connection between the two sets of problems and thus perceive the emotional depths of the novels may erroneously believe that Raskin is too exclusively "cerebral."

The pictures in Raskin's *Songs of Innocence* reflect, as did the drawings for Herrick, the timeless aspects of the poems and the degree to which the "angel with the bright key" was accepted as a solution to the children's problem in Raskin's own vision. The idea is explored further in *Figgs & phantoms*. Although not conventionally religious, Raskin appears in her Blake speech, as in these illustrations, to find mystical beliefs a comfortable aspect of daily life. Since Blake also, in her terms and his, was "accepting of the wondrous," this seems quite reasonable.

The music, however, does reflect the pain that is missing from the illustrations in a typical Raskin division, and the invitation to invent one's own dynamics to bring out individual feelings intensifies this aspect of the accompaniments. If it is true that the world is a "comedy for those who think and a tragedy for those who feel," Raskin always appears to be responding to both worlds. Here she appears to be capturing both sides of Blake, but only the edition with the music, as well as the woodcuts, will have this wholeness of interpretation.

A Paper Zoo: A Collection of Animal Poems by Modern American Poets (1968), edited by Renée Karol Weiss, is an interesting and useful collection intended to introduce young children to modern poetry. In the Afterword to the book, Raskin said of her illustrations,

> In this book I consider literal interpretation unfair to the young reader who is learning to visualize abstract words. (At times it could be helpful to read a poem aloud to a child and have him verbalize the picture before he sees my illustration.) What I have attempted to do in my illustrations is to complement the poetry (from ear to eye) and decorate each page. There are sixteen different poets in this book and I have retained one style—free, loose drawings with tight textural decorations. A singular style provides consistency to an anthology; and this particular style, free and tight, to me is poetry.[4]

The drawings are of the animals in the poems, but they are nonnaturalistic and objective. In many cases the outline is filled in with fanciful swirling pictures that make the drawings look as

though they had been cut out of tapestry. Kenneth Patchen's
"Magical Mouse," though, does have internal sketches of the
maidens and birds it has eaten, and Randall Jarrell's mother bats
have their children clinging underneath, although both require a
careful examination of the pictures. They would not, I think, interfere with the visualization process Raskin was trying not to
interrupt, since they are decorative, not interpretive, as she intended. The fact that she should have so intended, however, appears unnecessarily to diminish the illustrator's role in the book
and make her contribution less rewarding for herself and perhaps
inevitably for the audience. Although what she wrote in the Afterword is in keeping with her refusal to illustrate her own
novels, so as not to interfere with the reader's imagination, Ardizzone's statement about illustrating poetry—"In all these books
the very sound of the words is evocative of pretty pictures. It is
as if the poems or stories take charge and illustrate themselves
and one's pen is only a medium for their self-expression"[5]—suggests a more confident and natural approach, as well as being
closer to the approach Raskin herself took in her earlier poetry
illustration. *Silly Songs and Sad,* a book of Raskin's own verse
with startlingly different styles of illustration at each spread, appeared the year before the Weiss collection, apparently conceived
in quite a different way. Although *A Paper Zoo* and *Come Along!*
(1969) were published one after the other, Raskin explained her
illustrations in vastly different ways in her notes to these volumes. The late sixties, in fact, were an experimental period for
Raskin, both in the styles she used and in her conception of the
role of the illustrator.

   D. H. Lawrence: Poems Selected for Young People (1967) is a
different but attractive book. The collection is mostly of Lawrence's animal poems, though it includes some on human relationships. Unlike Raskin's other illustrations, these sketches are
done in pen and ink, consisting of short lines drawn diagonally
from right to left, resembling the shadowy background in her
Cleaver illustrations (1967 and 1968) but with a hard rather than
soft line. Like Lawrence, she could portray animals very well: her
mosquito, hummingbirds, and elephants are memorable.

Rebecca Caudill's *Come Along!* is a haiku collection about seasons by an established children's writer. Although Caudill could have exerted unusual control over the illustrations, she gave Raskin rein, and was very pleased with her interpretation; it was a project that brought Ann Durell (later, Raskin's editor at Dutton) and Raskin together (Durell interview).

Raskin said of these illustrations in her notes to the text: "I wanted the reader to see beyond the boundaries of the book as I tried to complement the author's word images with acrylic paint on colored rice paper. By not painting edge to edge, by avoiding an exact sense of scale or proportion, by eliminating shadows and horizons, I have hoped to achieve, not a picture of a landscape, but, like the haiku, a moment in nature."[6]

She constructed her "moment" by juxtaposing the ingredients of the poems with a small girl and her younger brother who observe the moment. For example, her painting for the page that contains "We climb the long hill./Daisies detain us, and moss,/And fiddlehead ferns" (16) is illustrated on a twilight blue background that extends across the fold onto the white poetry side. It is a fantastic mixture of daisies and fiddleheads in the foreground, with a red ladybug. Over the top of the middle daisies is the girl—arms forward around her little brother, who comes up to her chin—observing the flowers from a distance. With the children in the middle, the reader's eye pauses at the "moment in nature."

Goblin Market (1970) by Christina Rosetti (whose life and poetry Raskin later discussed in *the tattooed potato*) is another major Raskin project that took an unusually long time to conceive and illustrate. The poem concerns two sisters, Lizzie and Laura, who are tempted by goblin men to linger in the twilight and eat their goblin fruit. Raskin edited this edition herself, leaving out "197 lines, mostly self-contained units consisting of two minor themes: the death of Jeannie and the planting of the kernel stone."[7] In the afterword to the volume, she said that she did this because she felt that this poem, a personal favorite, was "too long for the contemporary reader and contained too many outdated Victorian proprieties."

The illustrations are elaborate. Raskin said that she spent

eight months sketching from early Italian frescoes and German engravings to get the flavor of the pre-Raphaelites (Dante Gabriel Rossetti, Christina's brother, did the first illustrations) without the actual Victorian style, and finally painting the illustrations in watercolor with fine pen line. She said, "My daughter posed for both girls. She is tall and straight and provided backbones to the usually languid Victorian maidens." The pictures flow across the pages, assisted by wreaths of flowing tresses and cascades of fruit.

Despite the book's meticulous professionalism, however, the illustrations diminish the effect of the poem seriously. It is tempting to think that Raskin's view of the "Victorian proprieties" is at the root of the problem and may result from the disengagement of heart and head in her interpretation of the poem.

At the heart of any interpretation of the strange and provocative poem is the feeling that the goblin fruit is an objective correlative for some experience that the sisters desired but were denied. Although the plot shows us one sister rescuing the other from a deathlike state brought on by eating the forbidden fruit and then finding that she cannot have any more, the fruit still seems desirable; life without it seems dull. Raskin appears to be taking this into account when she leaves a little goblin alone in the last page at a time when he is supposed to have been vanquished for good, "Whether this is to compensate for the loss of the goblins or to continue their menace is a choice I leave to the reader." In spite of understanding the lasting appeal of the goblin fruit, which many interpreters, indeed, have missed, Raskin appears to have left out of her sunny pictures the power and nature of the desire and its fatal consequences. Rossetti's poem was written for children, but it is the sort of poem for children that perhaps only a Victorian could write. The desire for goblin fruit is a desire linked, persuasively, with the uncanny desire for fairyland,[8] but also with insatiable hunger, sexual desire, sexual freedom, and freedom, itself. (Students today often think of drug addiction as the "goblin fruit.") Lizzie, with her Christ-like willingness to sacrifice for her sister, rescues the fallen Laura from a state that would seem to be desirable—that is, eating the luscious goblin fruit—if only the fruit did not cause the maiden to lose her maidenhood and ability to live on in her maiden world. The poem's power comes from its sensual, erotic imagery; obviously, it is a difficult poem to illustrate for children.

Death (which is what befell Jeannie, who was left out by Raskin), insatiable craving, and erotic animal furriness is simply not summed up by the Raskin goblins, who appear as cheerful little grotesques in period costume. Raskin did not want the goblins to be frightening, but things that can kill *must* be frightening. If the goblins are not frightening, the poem lacks tension.

Raskin probably felt, rightly, that Victorian prohibitions about sexuality were outdated. She might have felt that her own daughter was growing up in a world that allowed stronger women's roles and new freedom to express them. Although Raskin herself married several times briefly when another might simply have had affairs, Turtle's views on her sister's rather archaic marriage plans in *The Westing Game* seem to give the view that sexuality had changed in the seventies. But taking away the intellectual reason for the sisters' dilemma does not solve the emotional message of the poem: Goblin fruit remains powerfully desirable and absolutely forbidden, or else the poem does not make sense.

Raskin is to be thanked for giving the poem a format appropriate for children (Rosetti's intended audience). She successfully gave us the upright, loving Lizzie who saved her Laura—"For there is no friend like a sister, / In calm or stormy weather"—and she underscored the appeal of goblin men. She went astray when she felt that the aspects of "Goblin Market" that we all feel can be illustrated in the clear, daylight world of her watercolors or that banishing Victorian prudery banishes the dangers of goblin fruit.

Raskin's most beautiful work is included in these illustrations for the work of others. Her woodcuts, in particular, are memorable and rich, though she worked well in a variety of media, as this collection reflects. Except for the illustrations of Mona in *Figgs &*

phantoms, Raskin's work for her own books is witty, rather than beautiful. Her warmest pictures, thérefore, accompany other people's texts and portray other people's feelings.

Raskin responded intelligently to text; her illustrations offer thoughtful thematic interpretations of her material, often encapsulating an interpretation of a whole within a single picture. Like Sendak, she illustrated well for Ruth Krauss's innovative work, which, in this case, was close to her own interest in perception and appearance. Although her own pleasure in the creative process is evident, however, Raskin's main concern always appears to have been to enhance the understanding and pleasure of the reader without interfering with the reader's own imaginative faculty. She retained memories of her own childhood responses to illustration and worked to surprise and satisfy that child.

3

Picture Books
"Words aren't everything"

In 1966 Ellen Raskin began preparing two books simultaneously: *Songs of Innocence* and *Nothing Ever Happens on My Block*. The Blake book was a project for Doubleday in her original woodcut style and was a timeless, beautiful composition. *Nothing Ever Happens on My Block* was an experiment with something new, submitted to Jean Karl at Atheneum. Raskin mentioned in several interviews that she was highly uncertain about the style of *Nothing Ever Happens*. In an interview with Jim Roginski, for example, she said, "I kept asking myself the whole time why I was doing *Nothing Ever Happens on My Block* because it was so cartoony and the Blake book was very arty" (Roginski, 169).

In 1979, at a workshop for teachers and librarians who hoped to become more comfortable describing illustration for book reviews, Raskin instructed the participants never to use the word "cartoon." She told them that it had become pejorative and that the general public and the professional artist meant different things by it. The cartoonist, she said, has mastery of line (a term of high praise), but it may not sound like high praise in a review. Raskin's "cartoon" style, then, was initially a departure for her, which ran counter to her training in the fine arts. But it became her trademark in the books she illustrated for herself. *Nothing Ever Happens on My Block* won the *Herald Tribune* Award for the best picture book of 1966, and, as Raskin said, "All of my energies had gone into *Songs of Innocence,* which went out of print very quickly, and *Nothing Ever Happens on My Block* is still doing well."[1]

The cartoon-style drawings for picture books were successful for significant reasons. Raskin is writing humor, intellectual humor, and line drawings are appropriate to her witty text. She is not primarily interested in portraying mood in her own picture books, although she did this sensitively for other authors. Similarly, the picture is telling the story in a picture book, and her picture books, like her novels, often concern a puzzle or something that must be investigated in the picture itself. The simplicity of the cartoon-style drawings encourages and facilitates discovering the multiple levels of the story. Most important, cartoons distance us from the scenes they portray, as does Raskin's nonnaturalistic use of color. Raskin's humor depends upon and creates this distance.

Stories about People, Society, and Perception

The joke on Chester Filbert is, of course, that he is dissatisfied with his neighborhood and life because "nothing ever happens" in it, when to the reader his neighborhood appears to be not only very attractive and worth getting to know, but extremely eventful. While he mopes on the curb thinking of the things that won't happen here, he is missing all kinds of wonderful action. The neighborhood is urban and very grand. The houses are Victorian mansions with lots of windows, floors, and ornamentation. The houses are done in black and white line with much detail, so the eye is drawn to Chester, also in black, who is a simple form in the right foreground, a position William Moebius suggests is related to low spirits and lack of security.[2] The neighbors and events are solid forms in color superimposed on the houses, with their remarks shown in cartoon balloons.

What Chester misses behind and around him are a number of engrossing sequences. Children repeatedly ringing the doorbell of a lady with knitting so annoy the lady that she ends up pouring water on the next person who rings, who happens to be the postman. A man digging a hole to plant a tree digs up a series of wonderful objects, ending with an Aladdin's lamp. The tree grows and bears fruit. A robber is chased by police. A girl who is in a skip-rope contest trips and breaks her arm and reappears in a cast; a house is repaired, destroyed by lightning, and repaired again. Housepaint mysteriously changes color, and an umbrella sprouts flowers. The rooster weathervane flies to a new house; a witch keeps appearing in different windows, an armored truck is struck by a motorist, and $50 bills float around in the air; Chester's cat, her new kittens, and his mother fail to get his attention. Perry Nodelman, in *Words about Pictures,* reminds us that Chester's world is a soundless, timeless picture-book world, or car crashes, for example, surely would have upset his despondent reverie. It is an additional irony in the story.[3]

Chester, with whom Raskin identified, is in a classic human situation. The strength of the story, after all, comes from its basic truth—what we get out of life depends on how actively we pursue it as well as on the range of our interests and the sensitivity of our perceptions. We feel sorry for Chester, and take heed of his example, when we perceive that he could have been having a memorable, never-to-be-forgotten day if he had looked up from the street in front of him.

Chester's neighborhood is a mixture of fantasy and reality that is believable because of its style and setting. Gingerbread houses with cupolas and widow's walks look magical to many people. The cartoon simplification predisposes us to the unusual and automatically suspends our disbelief. On the other hand, this also significantly reduces our emotional reaction to what is happening and forces us to see it as an intellectual problem: Robbers, auto accidents, lightning fires, broken arms, and neighborhood quarrels all have violent and upsetting possibilities, which are ignored here. They are only perceived as interesting, amusing incidents.

Raskin's story is realistic. Clearly, any neighborhood, known as a Harriet-the-Spy child knows it, is an engrossing study full of bizarre and hard-to-explain activities. Chester is wasting the only time in his life when he would be apt to know what goes on in the block so intimately. Raskin's neighborhood activities have a fey side to them, but a good many are the frustrating and difficult sort we associate with everyday existence. There is a high annoyance level here—the people trying to do home repairs and improvements continually see their work being undone and complicated by outside forces. The children and the lady are not examples of cooperation between generations. Transformed by humor, though, we recognize the incidents as things we would laugh at if we were told the stories: humor draws on human frustration, just as another person's catastrophe is apt to be our source of excitement and heady sense of importance. Hearing about someone else's broken arm *is* the sort of thing Chester would enjoy. The story is simple, but the elements of toughness and human truth are here, as is the beauty that Chester is missing in the natural world (the trees, flowers, kittens) and human relationships (friends, family). It is a perceptual problem with wide application.

The other books that feature Chester, *Spectacles* (1968) and *A & The* (1970), also explore ways of seeing. *Spectacles* is about Chester's friend Iris Fogel (her name is a pun on "focal"), whose visual problem (myopia) prevents her from seeing what is around her. As Eric A. Kimmel perceptively noted in his review for *Twentieth-Century Children's Writers*, Raskin's best work is tied to the problem of vision, and Chester and Iris have nearly opposite problems.[4]

The difference between Iris and Chester is that Iris has advanced beyond Chester in applying her imagination to life. Iris's nearsighted visions are more interesting than reality. Although she clearly needs spectacles for a portion of her life (the portion in which she is constantly scaring or offending her relatives, friends, and teachers), she retains the superiority of her myopic view by being able to take the spectacles off when she wants to. Raskin was, of course, myopic herself. She said her art did not develop until she could see the details; her reading, however, developed because books were all she *could* see, and it is reading that feeds the imagination.

Illustration from *Spectacles* by Ellen Raskin. © 1968 by Ellen Raskin. Reprinted by permission of Atheneum Publishers, an imprint of Macmillan Publishing Co. Original artwork for cover reproduced from the original illustration in the Kerlan Collection, University of Minnesota.

The picture book illustrations show Iris in black and white cartoon on the left side on white paper, balanced against her visions on consecutive pages: the nearsighted vision is smoky grey on boldly colored sheets (the chestnut mare), followed by the "real" picture, which is a detailed line drawing in three colors on white paper (babysitter with intricately covered sofa and floppy sanseveria). The "real" picture has its own, different, interest.

Little Chester in *Nothing Ever Happens* can imagine what he would like to see on his block, but he does not get the benefit of it because it makes him dissatisfied with what really is likely to go on, which, in Raskin's vision, is vivid and amazing. To complete the process, he should be able to see his own world well and also imagine better for when the world falls short. The goal is to be happy, after all. Iris has transformed fuzziness and gray shapes into an interesting world by her superior ability to mold her reality into something better. She is not dissatisfied with the result—she has achieved her own goal—it is the other people who complain. Raskin's book, which superficially resembles those problem books designed to make a child happy about new glasses, is revolutionary and sophisticated in theme. Like the best books anywhere, it insists on the legitimacy of the creative imagination and the insufficiency, at times, of reality. It also deals frankly with the problem that the person with a different perception is likely to have in life; Iris's social relations are funny, but rocky.

It is worth noting that although Raskin identified with both of these characters, Iris's position on the left side of the double spreads is the one with which we are most likely to empathize (Nodelman, 135), while Chester's is an insecure and arguably un-likable position on the far right (Nodelman, for example, dislikes him). Secondary characters in most of Raskin's picture books are sources of tension, as is clear from these examples, but the fact that the reader's sympathy is not automatically engaged for the main character makes her books decidedly unusual.

A & The; or, William T. C. Baumgarten Comes to Town tries to do too many things at once, but it is interesting. *A & The* has the *a*'s and *the*'s in boldface so that they can be picked out by all be-ginning readers. There is also some stressing of colors (orange tree, blue suit) in the story, which the learner might also recog-nize. Of course, such a child is not able to read the rest of the story, and one can see that picking out the letters and colors ought to be done before the reading of the page starts, or it will be dis-tracting. On the other hand, the typeface is worth looking at, and the variety of *a*'s and *the*'s, the italics, the type symbols, and vi-sual puns are a pleasure.

The experienced reader is presented with a simple neighbor-hood story with elaborate visual ramifications. William T. C. Baumgarten is the new child in the neighborhood, and Horace and Doris (from *Ghost in a Four-Room Apartment*), Morris, and Luke are reluctant to welcome him, even though he has a bike that Luke would like to borrow. The neighborhood is drawn like Chester's, but it is less grand. The apartment houses end at the sidewalk, with fire hydrants and canvas canopies over doorways. The buildings are brick and stone and not so fancy as those in Chester's neighborhood. The windows, however, still frame their own vignettes. An artist, the neighbors of a trombone player, and a penthouse owner gardening on the roof pursue their sometimes-surprising lives throughout the children's encounter.

When the newcomer gets to school, however, the teacher's lesson on the invasion of England in 1066 alters the children's vision of William T. C. Baumgarten. The lesson appears in a cartoon balloon over the schoolroom scene (which includes Chester and Iris Fogel as pupils), done in replicas of the Bayeux Tapestry! Reality is a little strained at the idea that so young a class is being taught from a text on the Battle of Hastings and the Domesday book. However, the emphasis on an eight-year-old duke is suitable. It is satisfying to see little William, whose initials are now revealed to stand for "The Conqueror," take his place in the Bayeux Tapestry of his new friends' imagination.

The book's strengths lie in its personalization of history when presenting Duke William as a child and the psychological realism of using the lesson as an excuse for the children to retreat from their standoffishness—a pose they had adopted out of shyness and little else. Luke is happy to get to ride the bike. The book's weakness lies mostly in the dialogue of the teacher and the heaviness of the historical text in contrast with the contemporary children's story, and also in the lack of action in a book that appears, unlike *Spectacles* and *Nothing Ever Happens,* to be a story rather than a discussion. Although this book could have been edited more skillfully, the idea still seems interesting and amusing and the Bayeux cartoon balloons are witty.

Ghost in the Four-Room Apartment (1969) and *Franklin Stein* (1972) are the last of the books that resemble these contemporary city stories. The story about the poltergeist extends the vision of life's possibilities and relationships. *Franklin Stein,* which with *Nothing Ever Happens* and *Spectacles* may be among Raskin's most lasting contributions to picture books, develops the perception theme significantly.

The poltergeist in *Ghost in the Four-Room Apartment* is repre-

Illustration from *A & The* by Ellen Raskin. © 1970 by Ellen Raskin. Reproduced from the original artwork by permission of the Kerlan Library, University of Minnesota.

sented by a text in white print on black pages. The alternating text is a rhyme about the relationships between the people who live in the apartment and all the relatives who are coming to dinner. These are done in ordinary black on a white page. The book's dedication page suggests (twice) that the book be read aloud in two voices. The black and white pages alternate with a double spread of the four rooms of the apartment with poltergeist activities going on in them, bewildering the family connection. Raskin uses color in a nonnaturalistic way to differentiate between the four rooms: Everything in the bedroom is the same green with detailed black ink drawing, and everything in the living room is blue. As in the other outside city pictures, important characters and details (flying blocks, smashing groceries, father in a flying rocking chair) are done in contrasting colors and appear to be superimposed on the background color.

The poltergeist, who claims to be a friend of Horace Homecoming ("Here is Horace, good and bad, / Who lives in a four-room apartment"), is looking through the cupboards for mustard pickles and smashing things up pretty thoroughly. In the pictures, Horace, who was initially reading a ghost story and is startled for a few pages, takes most of the shenanigans in stride, calmly eating flying fruit as his family attempts to get out of the chandelier and blames some of the mischief on Horace. He is rescued when the ghost leaves as the best-loved family member arrives ("Here is Boris, / Whose favorite is Horace. / Guess who he might be!"). The book ends with Horace hugging his grandpa in the midst of harried family activity.

The joke in *Ghost* comes in the contrast between the narrative voice that is reciting a humdrum rhyme about the family, apparently unaware of what is happening to that family, and the wild, naughty poltergeist's bizarre shouts and destructive activities. Horace's lack of reaction to the situation and the peculiar way the fruit and family are stuck up in the air are also funny, but the ghost is the most sympathetic and only active character. As a contribution to Raskin's view of perception, the poltergeist is invisible in the pictures, but his activities are not. His personality is made substantive in words, however, since he owns the white-on-black pages.

The greatest tension in the book lies in the hidden relation between Horace and the ghost. As in traditional poltergeist lore, the ghost appears to the adult, at least, to have been conjured up by Horace's unhappiness with his family or crowded living conditions in the apartment, a tension only temporarily palliated by the ending.

Franklin Stein uses the problem of perception more satirically and cynically than in the previous "vision" works. The characters of Franklin and Fred, however, are engagingly drawn and have the sympathy of the reader, while the ending promises a happier and funnier future than does *Ghost* or *Nothing Ever Happens*. These warm qualities make it enjoyable to a broader audience.

As we might guess in Iris's and Horace's cases, Franklin is identified as a friendless child who perceives life in a way at odds with the people around him. He is an artist who makes a wonderful monster creature to enter in a pet contest because the mean landlady won't let her boarders have any pets.

Like Horace's world, Franklin's is filled with people, none of whom seem very attractive. The landlady is mean and "too rich" to live in the house she rents out; the neighbors are "too busy" fighting, "being beautiful," "worrying about robbers," "singing duets," and "coming and going and working" to care about others. Franklin, on the other hand, has the gentle sweetness of Augie in *The Mysterious Disappearance of Leon (I Mean Noel)*, and his monster, Fred, is gentle and loopy, too, with window blinds swooping around his shoulders. Fred really existed. Raskin's husband and son-in-law gathered her the materials to build him, and her drawings were taken from a real model. The house is Victorian, crowded, and falling apart. It and the landlady are done in the same green and aqua. Fred is completely red in every picture, so the color identifies and locates him.

Franklin's lonely state is emphasized by the public reaction when he brings Fred out into the world to go to the contest. Franklin is lonely, but he is always lonely in a crowd. There is no empty space or sterile desert in a Raskin book. For example, on the way to the contest, the landlady's conviction that Fred is "wicked" is echoed by every passerby. "Two tow-truck drivers and the other grown-ups agreed. They had never seen anything quite like Fred, so he must be wicked, indeed, or worse." The cartoon balloon captions read: "Awful," "sinister," "atrocious," "ferocious," and "weird." But after the judges have declared Fred the winner of the Most Unusual Pet prize and declare the creation "original," "creative," "artistic," and "superb," everyone agrees with the judges. Fortunately, Franklin's experience of the ignorant public's fickle reception of artists is not the only thing he gains on his excursion. He also finds a friend, "Elizabeth, who made things, too," and the last scene shows them ordering up body parts at the local butcher's shop.

Like *Spectacles,* Franklin's story champions the imaginative vision and shows a child turning an unsatisfactory life into something better through that vision. But where Chester (and the people who aren't nearsighted) were perceived as merely unfortunate because of their limitations, here, as Franklin's public, they have a significantly bad impact on the artist's life. They are also foolish for being afraid of the new and for following other people's judgments mindlessly. Raskin pursues this theme again in her novel about art, *the tattooed potato & other clues,* published the next year, but she is really most severe on the public in the picture book. The didacticism of the text attracted some criticism, yet it is hard to know whether the same charge might not always eliminate satire from the children's picture book genre. Satiric humor is not at all common in children's books, and not all of the reasons for rejecting it are defensible.

Raskin's harshest view of humanity, however, appeared in a book in 1971, the year before *Franklin Stein* was published. *The World's Greatest Freak Show* is not one of the contemporary city books; its illustrations place the setting in a highly colored landscape of fantastic antiquity. Like Raskin's Depression novel, *The Mysterious Disappearance,* it concerns poverty and the unwise and desperate things people will do to escape it. Raskin once said that she thought that *The World's Greatest Freak Show* was all her meanness coming out. It would be more accurate, I think, to characterize it as an overflowing of indignation about social discrimination. The "meanness" is surely discouragement that the world is so cruel to those who are different. The satiric intention, political reference, and strong moral, however, are more pronounced than in the other books.

Like the pictures in *Goblin Market,* those in *Freak Show* use historic costume. The costumes suggest a medieval or renaissance context, with castle-like structures and jerkins, mixed with contemporary references, sofas and interiors. The "Tizuvthee" (as in "My country, 'tis of thee") residents, like the goblins, are mixtures of distorted human and animal shapes. The pictures are line drawings flowing across double spreads, with the groups of people, water, hillside villages and so on dominating the pages. The colors are pink, violet, aqua, green, and yellow—an almost-fluorescent palette for a gaudy moral tale.

Alastair Pflug is a kind of artist (a magician) who fails to develop his gift because of his vanity and because it is his primary desire to become rich and famous, not good at the art. By coldhearted maneuvering, he gets a chance at success in the country Tizuvthee across the sea and assembles a group of "freaks" as an attraction. The enormously fat person, the person with feathers, and the person with two heads (Jean-Jacques Cornflake) are miserable, but they need money badly. The plan backfires on the repulsive, dapper Alastair (who trips about in little boots with golden curls) when it becomes clear that his "freaks" look just like all the other people in Tizuvthee, and they settle down to a happy life. Alastair's appearance, though, is markedly odd in this society, so he grows rich and unhappy being a bad magician whose appearance draws hooting, ogling crowds at every performance.

Like the illustrations for *Shrieks at Midnight,* the individuals in the pictures are remarkably harsh and grotesque. Their hair and clothing contain many tight curls and flowing internal lines, which Moebius calls capillarity (151), and the faces, disconcertingly, are frequently looking in different directions. The tension caused by these elements is appropriate, of course, to a jeering, ogling populace, and the diffused attention is realistic.

Raskin's meticulous balance of her pages contributes to the satiric tone of the book. The picture of the ship going across the sea, for example, seems to be pressing against itself and the text in something like the tension that Raskin described in her *Paper Zoo* illustrations. The emphasis in the picture is not on the characters on the boat, but on the vast sweep of flowing water leading to the silhouette of Tizuvthee in the bottom right-hand corner. The grace and balance of the composition seems to diminish the plight of the characters, as indeed, the text does (the page includes a silly attempt to sound nautical on the part of Alastair). But the sharp edges of the fluid element, and the many intertwining billows, show the tension in the story. The tension is not resolved because the basic pessimism about flawed human nature remains at the end. Although Raskin created a persona whose features are often recognized in our society as appropriate for moral heroes and showed this perception to be entirely false, she did not produce anyone with superior qualities to leaven the message. The Tizuvthee people are just as intolerant of difference as Alastair is.

Raskin discussed discrimination against those with unusual bodies in five of her books. Since Raskin kept her own serious, but invisible, disease a secret, perhaps the source of her interest concerned the victims' lack of control over how other people perceived them. Certainly, she entered on the "freak" material with much less self-consciousness than another person might have. Although one can certainly understand the reviewers' uncertainty about using "freak" material, Raskin does appear to be honest about our society. Raskin never wrote for children in a way that suggests that she thought children had different needs than adults; the assurance she gave at the end of her novels was a present for herself. *Freak Show* at least questions our society's beliefs about children's capacities and the degree to which we are willing that they should criticize our society.

As a picture book, *The World's Greatest Freak Show* was not and is unlikely to be popular. It is too grim to be funny, once one gets past the awesome awfulness of Alastair. As a continuation of the problem of vision, however, it goes a step beyond correctly perceiving physical reality to recognition of correct action. The artist's eye needs not only to note accurately what the appearance is, for honesty's sake, but also discount that appearance as a guide to how a person ought to be treated or evaluated. Imagination is useful here to gain insight into the plight of the oppressed, but the artist's eye is being called on to determine moral truths rather than simply physical ones.

Since a story told primarily through pictures is perhaps a difficult medium for making the point that appearance is not the way to judge others, Raskin was predictably less simple, less didactic, and more interesting when she approached a similar problem in the longer novel told entirely in words: *the tattooed potato*. The human problem presented there by Isaac Bickerstaffe (the mutilated, brain-damaged man in the basement) is more subtle than any in the picture books, and human frailty (even vanity or greed) is treated with more compassion. Raskin's works all explore appearance and vision to some extent. She worked out the role of the artist through many of her most productive years both as an illustrator and as a writer. Because it was more confrontational for Raskin to approach a problem in print, moral problems seem to be worked out with more freshness there.

Stories Mostly about Animals

Silly Songs and Sad (1967) is a book of verse published by Crowell the year after Raskin's success with *Nothing Ever Happens*. The verse is not distinguished, although the illustrations were often chosen individually as vignettes in literary publications and advertisements. The most unusual aspect of the book is that each poem is illustrated in a different style, ranging from reproductions of Chinese horses through something like Raskin's usual picture book style to ultramodern animals with thick black outlines and startling checked tablecloths. Probably the most familiar illustrations are Miss Anabel, who is shown crying while riding a carousel, and the happy little man shaped like a pear.

The use of a different kind of illustration on every page shows Raskin's versatility, as the verse shows her familiarity with traditional forms, but the overall effect in the book is bewildering.

Although Raskin was extremely fond of animals and zoos, the

fact that her last four picture books feature primarily animal pictures rather than pictures of children may be partly due to social criticism focused on the picture book industry in that era. Raskin's penchant for justice was clearly in harmony with the protests of the late sixties and seventies, but interpreting neighborhood children in illustration in a way that did not lead to misunderstanding and charges of racism was challenging. Although the animal books explore problems similar to those in the books with humans, they appear more remote from daily life and less substantive.

And It Rained (1969) presents the problem of how animals in a rain forest can have tea properly at four o'clock in the afternoon when it always rains at five minutes past. Although the story has three main characters, a pig, a potto, and a parrot, it features "an all-star cast" of 11 other animals who all live out their lives in the pictures and are accessible to the preliterate child.

The crowdedness of the rain forest is like the family crowdedness and city crowdedness of Raskin's other books. In the book about Chester, this human richness suggested opportunities he ought to be having. This view stayed with Raskin, who perpetually keeps life lively and bizarre in her books through the variety and bounce of her characters. But the other animals also add perspective. The three friends are making a terrific fuss, but their neighbors are entirely unmoved by the problem. Perhaps they are heartless, and perhaps the problem doesn't deserve their concern.

The presentation of the plot is nonnaturalistic, both in text and illustration. The rain forest is stylized and park-like in gentle blues and greens that reverse when it starts and stops raining. The complaints and attitudes are recognizable to anyone who has worked on a problem with a committee, but the actual speech is in a repeated refrain, which distances it from reality. The focus, therefore, is on the number of ways the tea-in-the-rain problem can be approached and solved.

Like *The World's Greatest Freak Show, Moe Q. McGlutch, He Smoked Too Much* (1973) caused some critical doubt about Raskin's choice of material. Some reviewers assumed that the book was intended, or perhaps commissioned, as an antismoking tract.

Such a goal is unlikely to produce good literature—however desirable a nonfiction pamphlet on the topic might be—and is properly questioned. But the theme of the work is not that smoking is bad, and it seems doubtful that smoking was important or central to Raskin's intentions. Indeed, since Raskin herself smoked, it seems a peculiar moral for her to choose.

Moe Q. McGlutch, illustrated differently from any other Raskin book, has beautifully finished, smoky pictures without line but with sharp edges. It appears as if painted material might have been cut out to make this appearance. The pictures are sophisticated and, characteristically, contain more than the text tells. The story concerns the visit of a family of zebras to the home of a rich, important donkey whom the zebra parents are anxious to impress. The child has been, inevitably, instructed to be as flattering and obsequious as the parents but keeps telling the host that he smokes too much, which is true. The smoking causes accidents, fires, absurd difficulties, and only the child—like Andersen's child in *The Emperor's New Clothes*—tells the truth about the matter. He is rewarded for this in the host's will.

Since nothing is mentioned about emphysema, or, indeed, anything bad that would happen to a normal smoker, the issue appears to be much more the importance of honesty, the wisdom of the innocent child, or, more likely, the absurdity of people who tell lies and behave in an undignified way to curry favor—a theme that echoes *Freak Show*. The parents are the villains because their values are misplaced; Moe Q. McGlutch is a villain because he is insensitive to other people's feelings until he finally gets the point (too late). Both satirical points are obvious and funny in the text.

Moe Q. McGlutch contains several interesting stylistic departures for Raskin. First, she greatly expands the technique of using the same figures several times in the same double spread to indicate the different steps of the narrative or other action features. This gives the book a witty and rollicking effect and adds movement and liveliness.

Second, she does more here with the nature of the animals she uses in their relation to the people they represent in the story.

Moe's donkey nature is an extension of traditional braying donkey stereotype: his unpleasant teeth and gums are prominent since the focus is on his smoking habit, and his persistence and insensitivity are blockheaded. His assertion of leadership and generous sociability, however, make him more interesting than other Raskin picture-book villains and more droll than evil. The zebras are amusing because they do un-zebralike activities: riding bicycles, for example, a hard thing for zebra legs to do. However, Little Zeke's figure is very childlike and warmly emotional for a Raskin picture. His potbelly, childlike energetic posture when sitting and wistfulness when all the balloons get blown up convey his vulnerability to crazy adult activities and give depth to the story. Although other characters change their garments and colors during the story, Zeke's sweater is always yellow, the color traditionally associated with cheer.

Third, the surprises in *Moe Q. McGlutch* have narrative as well as perceptual importance. The viewer can see smoke rings coming from a room in the onion-domed mansion at the time the zebras are approaching up the hill for their visit, for example, but the smoke can easily be ignored or considered a stylized cloud until the third opening in which the smoke coming from a hole in the bedroom ceiling explains Moe's presence on the zebras' counterpane. Similarly, green swirls in the water or green scales sneaking around the tree after the auto accident might simply be artistic fanciness. But one is later revealed to be a sea monster who objects to having ashes dropped on him, and the other is the smoke-eating dragon that follows Moe home from the zoo—a fact not revealed in text until three openings later.

It is a challenge to keep up with these pictures, since they do not have the simplicity of Raskin's line drawings. There are witty allusions like the unicorn in the zoo who is borrowed from the unicorn tapestry. There are also tricks that involve not knowing when an action has occurred because of the stopped effect of the picture. For example, when Moe breaks two of Zeke's balloons on sequential pages about the zoo, we do not know until the second picture on the page in which Zeke holds a limp scrap of rubber that the accident was going to occur—was, indeed, occurring right that minute. On first glance, we interpret the first picture as Moe standing in front of Zeke and the balloons, a combination of smokiness and perspective; in the second such picture we ought to already know the joke. However, the scene portrayed is one we cannot see in real life. In real life we do not see the balloon as whole and round at the moment the cigarette penetrates the rubber. This can happen only in a picture, and it extends the joke.

Thus, although *Moe Q. McGlutch* has a strong satiric message and a misleading name, the prominence of the humor, the degree to which we are made to empathize with the finally triumphant child, the interesting narrative, and the more rounded character of the villain make it an attractive book.

Who, Said Sue, Said Whoo? (1974), *Moose, Goose, and Little Nobody* (1974), and *Twenty-Two, Twenty-Three* (1976) are all searches. *Who, Said Sue, Said Whoo?*, which received the most attention and prizes, is a cumulative rhyme book in which Sue, a little girl with a knit cap and a roadster, is searching for an animal who remains missing until the end. The animal says "chitter, chitter, chatter," but the moral points out that words aren't everything: the animal is a skunk.

The pictures are extremely attractive, and their elegance explains the critical acclaim. Line drawings flow across the opening; the animals have the same graceful shapes as those in *And It Rained*. The odd assortment all gets in the small car while Sue continues driving. They refuse as a group to react to any misfortune up to the arrival of the smelly skunk. The vegetation is extraordinary. The corn, artichokes, and mushrooms are exaggerated and stylish, the leaves on the tree are luxuriant and full. The book is a little game rather than a story. It introduces the next animal to be guessed somewhere in the preceding picture, so that the prereader can watch for the new one in the illustrations. These pictures, though more interesting in themselves than as narrative, are vintage Raskin: the crowdedness and exuberance, the wild mixture of animals and vegetation from different temperate zones and a billy goat's ghost with the living characters, and the cool acceptance of the heroine when gnus climb in the vehicle and oaks crash down on the hood. All Raskin heroines can put up with a great deal when they have a mystery (even a very little one) to solve.

Moose, Goose, and Little Nobody is a search that shares something with *The Mysterious Disappearance of Leon (I Mean Noel).* Mrs. Carillon's search in that book is decidedly unconventional because she has not been educated. She is ignorant of the ordinary way of doing things and uses her own original ideas to search, instead. It takes her longer, but it gets her farther. Moose and Goose are considerably sillier than Mrs. Carillon, but their ignorance (which ought, in this case, to make the child feel superior) is similarly at the heart of the search. A young mouse is blown away on a roof in a storm, and the two friends (clothed animals of friendly disposition) promise to find his name, his house, and his mother. Goose can read, but she doesn't know what animals are called (other people would know a mouse is a mouse). The animals are looking for a house without a red roof, but they identify phone books and buses as likely candidates: they do not consult size when they guess, nor do they seem to be able to compare the appearance of one animal with that of another. This is some kind of perceptual problem; they either have vision without judgment or a deficiency in processing details, rather like the one afflicting Oliver Sacks's man who mistook his wife for a hat. Because the theme of being restored to home rather than rebelling against it seems to be remote from Raskin's deepest needs, it is tempting to blame lack of conviction on Raskin's part for the odd nature of this text.

Twenty-Two, Twenty-Three, the last picture book and the penultimate book published in Raskin's lifetime, is astonishing in many ways. Although it departs from her earlier styles, its beautiful finish and execution are far too assured to be called experimental. The endpapers are green maps showing (in the front) the mouse's solitary pilgrimage through the countries where she got her varied wardrobe (sari, muumuu, etc.) and (in the back) her proposed travels with the dove. The inside of the endpaper has a sign pointing forward to the half title page and back to the front cover and book jacket. The half title features the mouse with suitcase and her future friend the dove on a sign pointing to the title

page. The copyright page and the dedication pages here are used
to introduce characters and action.

All the pages are rimmed by a narrow black line border, unlike
Raskin's other illustrations. Raskin uses the border classically, to
separate the picture from life. The characters walk on the border
and hang from the top: the border establishes that the characters
are pictures and that they are somehow circumscribed by the
pages of the book. They exist on the pages, themselves, not in the
world of imagination. The mouse's first question—"Pardon me,"
said the traveling mouse, "but what is this and where are we?"—
reinforces the role of page as place. The title refers to *pages* 22
and 23 in the book.

On the other hand, the characters' ability to "live" on the pages
gives the pages more than expected importance. Ordinarily, one
cannot take a trip to a book in the sense that one can arrive on a
page of it and walk through it to the end. Without mentioning
magic, the traveling mouse is jumping into the book rather like
Bert did into his sidewalk chalk drawings in *Mary Poppins*.

The animals are drawn in a naturalistic style: ink line fully
filled in with hair, fur, and feathers. At the same time, their posture is human, and they wear odd human garments that rhyme
with each animal's name: a cock in a smock, snail in a veil, ram
in a tam. The story has two mysteries: What is "Twenty-two,
Twenty-three"? What item of clothing must the mouse put on in
order to become part of "Twenty-two, Twenty-three"? Most of the
text consists in the other animals' finding fault with the mouse's
clothes (some children might see that it has to rhyme), whereas
the dove keeps gently encouraging the mouse to try something
else. The illustrations are primarily black and white, but some
items in each picture are done in red, green, yellow and browns.
On pages 22 and 23, these items are finally pushed into position
as parts of a Christmas tableau and letters which spell "Merry
New Year." One needs to look back at the preceding pictures
to correctly identify the ingenious puzzle pieces (the ear of
an ape becomes Santa's mouth). Afterward, the mouse and dove
depart.

On one level, this does not seem the sort of book to become a perennial Christmas favorite since it does not exude traditional warmth and emotional content.

Oddly enough, though, *Twenty-Two, Twenty-Three* appears to have another kind of intensity. The combination of the dove and the brevity of the rhymed text suggests some metaphysical significance. It would be inappropriate to read specifically Christian symbolism into the text; the author did not come out of that tradition. But the fact that Raskin understood William Blake's ability to see angels at the dinner table (and had seen the prophet Elijah at her own) suggests that she realized the connections. *Twenty-Two, Twenty-Three* sounds like the adventures of a soul seeking union with mystical awareness—peculiar as this analysis undoubtedly sounds.

> "Pardon me,"
> said the traveling mouse,
>   "but what is this
> and where are we?"
>
> "It is not where we are,"
> said the ape in the cape,
> said the goat in the coat,
>   "it is where
>   and what
> we are going to be."
>
> "Below and above,"
> said the dove
> with gloves on his feet.

When the mouse departs from *Twenty-Two, Twenty-Three* with the dove, it is hard to believe that their next destination is *Texas,* as the endpapers suggest. Larger issues are being raised and more interesting destinations implied. In *Figgs & phantoms,* the pirate attempts to frighten Mona out of Capri with the sound of powerful lines from Milton. The power of rhyme and the absence of details also operates in *Twenty-Two, Twenty-Three,* putting portentousness into the holiday greeting.

Conclusion: "Words Aren't Everything"

Arnold Lobel said in his essay "A Good Picture Book Should . . .," "Not too many bad things happen in picture books. If they do, they usually find their way to a happy resolution at the end. I like them that way. When I feel the morbid need for unpleasantness and despair, I can read the newspaper or watch the news on television or just look out of my window. Picture books are a sanctuary from all of that."[5] Some of Raskin's picture books undoubtedly violate this precept, yet she would have agreed with Lobel about the need for escape from reality. Raskin was not herself a reader of children's literature nor a believer that children needed a different view of reality than the one suitable for adults. This is the difference. She would never have thought of a picture book for relief when "brought low by the vicissitudes of life" (Lobel, 75).

Raskin's need for escape can be seen in *Spectacles,* the book to which she felt closest, and *Franklin Stein.* She does not portray reality as pleasant in that book, but she shows how the use of the creative imagination can alter reality to something better. She honestly acknowledges that this is an escape; she never tries to make real life sound better than she herself perceived it to be. Beauty, in poetry, is what Raskin would have looked to instead of picture books, which is why her poetry illustration, with its eternal serenity, differs from her picture-book style. As her novels tell us, she also thought of art, games, and work as necessary to create one's own happiness, some of which are represented in the picture books she wrote. The escape she sought in books appears to have been of a particular nature. She was not looking for comfort but for something to stimulate her imagination. She could say, I think, that in spite of her lack of reassurance, she regularly provided original, interesting books.

It is hard to know exactly how far Raskin realized that her books were sometimes satiric and showed humanity and family members as flawed and oppressive. She said that she felt she owed children honesty, but, as Kimmel suggested (639), her intentions often appear to be the intellectual goal of exploring perception or solving a mystery; nor were the tension and worry mentioned by her reviewers, who evidently did not perceive them. At the Berkeley Symposium she mentions in "Me and Blake," she refused to be considered a fantasy writer, refused to talk about humor, and determined, after sharp discussion, that she was a smoking ethnic realist (351).

The pictures in Raskin's picture books appear to carry most of the book's appeal and message. Raskin's text is often verse or near-verse with repetition or refrains offering structure. There is little dialogue or textual humor. The humor is visual.

The absence of dialogue points to a characteristic of Raskin picture books that some critics have paused over—the fact that unusual and fascinating characters may be introduced but that no climax or important action follows to further explain them. Raskin stories have logical endings; she finishes what she started. But story was not her issue. It would be more appropriate to look at many of the Raskin books as essays or nonfiction investigations of ideas: what is finished is not the character's life and living, but the working out of the ramifications of the idea. The character needs no intricate personality, because he or she generally only represents a point of view.

What attracts Raskin's readers is the sophistication and style of the illustrations and the varied nature of the material she presented. Her books are original, and her voice is never condescending. She was not approaching an age group so much as a kind of reader (her kind) who would appreciate her wit and alienated, offbeat viewpoint in a visual format.

When Ann Durell asked Raskin to try a longer novel, something about her childhood during the Depression, she was thinking specifically about Raskin's gift for telling funny anecdotes. It was a request that also coincided with Raskin's increasing physical difficulty with her hands, which suggested the need for a new creative outlet. But it might well be the response of anyone who has paused over one of the Raskin picture books about children and has seen that the neighborhood vignettes, the family members, and the family relations are glimpses of situations that must have been much more realized in the illustrator's mind as she made them.

Raskin did not like to see illustrations in a novel because she felt that they would interfere with the reader's imagination. Therefore, when she turned to the writing of a long story, the fecundity and absurdity seen in the illustrations was directed exclusively to text. Because the desire for story, on the whole, is the strongest human need and because writing about a problem was a harder activity for Raskin than graphically presenting it, the Raskin novels appear to complete and refine the investigations that the picture books start.

4

The Mysterious Disappearance
of Leon (I Mean Noel)

Two corned beef sandwiches, lean, and don't forget
the pickles.
                              (apparent response to prayer)[1]

Ellen Raskin greatly admired Henry James, whose first editions
she collected. Mrs. Carillon, the deserted bride and soup heiress
of *The Mysterious Disappearance,* has a likeness to James's young
women setting foot for the first time on European soil: she is
young, unconventional, true, and has an unfaithful husband.
Mrs. Carillon also has the romantic innocence of Huck Finn because she, too, was never properly educated and therefore never
ruined by socialization. She is a tabula rasa (or its equivalent in
asterisks, as the clever illustrations in *The Mysterious Disappearance* make clear); this is the reason for her unusual approach
to finding her lost husband, Leon (or Noel) Carillon.

Oddly, this book appears to be Raskin's response to her editor's
request for an autobiographical novel. The fantastic and silly subject matter does not, of course, literally recount her life. The story
begins on a Thanksgiving Day when "poverty had spread
throughout the land": Two neighboring farm families, the Fishes
and the Carillons, too poor to have a good traditional dinner,
make soup out of their remaining food (tomatoes and potatoes) to
make the best of the situation. The soup, which eventually eases

the plight of the hungry at 10 cents a can and makes millions for the soup-makers, tragically alters the destiny of the two children of the families. Because no one can decide whose name should be put on the soup, they marry five-year-old Caroline Fish to seven-year-old Leon Carillon and call it "Mrs. Carillon's Pomato Soup." Then they promptly send Leon off to the Seymour Hall School for the rest of his childhood, get mean Miss Oglethorpe to oversee young Mrs. Carillon (one can't send a married woman to a nice school), and put all their efforts into soup-making.

Mrs. Carillon is the passive victim of circumstances until the day when the now-grown and orphaned couple meets at Palm Beach to leave their unhappy childhood behind for good. Unfortunately, the confusing meeting on the dock ends in a boating accident, in which Mrs. Carillon loses consciousness; when she awakens in the hospital, Leon (or Noel) is missing. Mrs. Carillon dedicates her life to finding the missing, and possibly amnesiac, Leon, and she is determined to do it her own way.

The story, which begins and ends at Thanksgiving meals, is measured out in a systematic and calculated way. For example, it is broken into three parts by the three times that Mrs. Carillon loses consciousness in the story. Mrs. Carillon's subjection to her childhood marriage is symbolically shown by her association with purple, starting with the purple flowered wedding dress made out of the Carillon tablecloth and ending with her achievement of a full life of her own, and a new wardrobe, at the end. In the Raskin cartoon illustrations that start each chapter, Mrs. Carillon's figure is always filled in with the asterisks that represent the purple flowers. Augie Kunkel, Mrs. Carillon's childhood friend and rescuer, enters her adult life to assist her search. His investigation and final solution is contained between two duck dinners.

Although *The Mysterious Disappearance* is a complex book, the difficulty of Raskin's subject matter is made more manageable by Raskin's patterning of the material. Raskin aimed at careful readers, but her book has no long, unbroken sections of text and looks unusually accessible. Every page is divided into her measured segments, and each contains such elements as lists, type changes, personal letters, and other breathing places to stop and think about the clues to Leon's whereabouts.

Since Raskin did not wish to illustrate her novels, she compromised by making decorative chapter pages illustrated by cartoon heads of the important characters. The characters' bodies are made out of words that summarize their position in the text. The word pictures clarify the text. One can see from their faces that Augie and Mrs. Carillon are nice and gentle; they are portrayed in plump, innocent cartoons. There is a contrast between Mrs. Carillon's picture and those of the others, which is thematically significant; and Mrs. Carillon looks decidedly eccentric when she ages yet preserves the same hairstyle and dress that she wore as a child.

Mrs. Carillon's mystery takes some of these explanations because it depends upon its heroine's character. If Mrs. Carillon had learned to reason systematically or to operate in the world at all, she might have found Leon (or Noel) fairly soon. But since she was left uneducated by the mean Miss Oglethorpe, as well as bruised and pinched, she works from two sets of words: the 14 postcards that Leon sent her from school during the 14 years of their marriage and the last words she heard from him as their boat went down at the dock at Palm Beach. Consulting the schoolboy notes for clues to his tastes and interests, she takes to watching cowboy movies, studying racing forms, and eating in Chinese restaurants. Piecing together phonics that might make sense of the last words she heard in the boat before she lost consciousness, she moves from city to city, investigating any place that might fill in the blanks and feeding seals at the zoo. The postcards and syllables, set out systematically with occasional hints from Raskin, provide the puzzle mystery at the heart of the novel.

Mrs. Carillon's search, while hilariously roundabout, is psychologically moving. She must find Leon, not only because she wants love but because she needs to overcome the effects of her early life before she can move on to be her own person: her future, as she sees it, is bound up with that of her lawful, though unchosen, husband. Her disappointed early hope of divine intervention in

Illustration from *The Mysterious Disappearance of Leon (I Mean Noel)* by Ellen Raskin. Text and illustrations © 1971 by Ellen Raskin. Reproduced by permission of the publisher, E. P. Dutton, a division of Penguin Books USA, Inc. Original illustration in the Kerlan Collection, University of Minnesota.

her plight does not cause her to lose her faith, but after she mistakes a delicatessen order for the voice of God, she never can bring herself to use the telephone again. Fortunately, Mrs. Carillon's search indirectly provides her with everything that her foolish family had denied her. Though she takes until middle age to do it, she finally finds her identity, two children, an education, a home in New York City, a useful role, and love.

American Dreams: Characteristic Motifs

Mrs. Carillon's life resembles, to some extent, Raskin's own. Raskin, too, had achieved this kind of personal success in her life and, like Mrs. Carillon, it took her some time and work to do it. But she was proud of her daughter, her final marriage to Dennis Flanagan was a successful one, and her free-lance career was based on hard work and talent like that of the artist (Joel Wells) in the novel. Like Tina and Tony, she had been unhappy because many moves made it difficult to make friends at school; like Christmas Bells, the racehorse, she had achieved a kind of fame "coming from nowhere." Although Mrs. Carillon's story coincides with Raskin's in many ways, it probably most parallels her young womanhood, when she was attempting to establish herself as an illustrator in New York City. Mrs. Carillon is rich, but her life has been warped and darkened by poverty; as such, she represents a type familiar in Raskin's work.

The World's Greatest Freak Show, also published in 1971, is another book that begins when poverty spreads over the land and deals with the cruel and humiliating things people are willing to do to get money when they haven't any. *The Westing Game,* which won the Newbery Medal, discusses the guilt of a man who founded a company and acquired great wealth, but neglected his family and cheated competitors. Although many literary works discuss the compromises between idealism and greed and the deleterious effects of money-grubbing, it is worthwhile to note that *Heart of Darkness* (which Uncle Flo tells Mona in *Figgs & phantoms* is one of his favorite stories) is a particularly strong fable on this subject from one of Raskin's favorite novelists. Conrad's Mr. Kurtz is the worst thing a person can be because he is willing to turn into a savage bent on murder and sadistic rites in the name of ivory-hunting. This was a strong theme for Raskin because making money was important to her. She was frightened terribly by the overnight poverty she experienced as a child in the Depression and worked very hard to make sure that she would not have to worry again in a similar way. This perspective on money and its relative importance in life is a perspective from a woman who had reason to know what the temptation to serve material needs at the expense of humane ones was like.

The approval that Raskin gives the protesters in *The Mysterious Disappearance* who try to free Mrs. Carillon from the Women's House of Detention and later organize the laborers in the soup factory is a family tradition and fundamental loyalty. Raskin's murdered grandfather, for whom she was named, was a member of the Industrial Workers of the World (IWW). But, as in *Westing Game,* which got away from her—"my tribute to American labor history ended up a comedy in praise of capitalism" ("Newbery", 390)—Raskin's views here are mixed. The soup factory, for instance, while it causes unnecessary sorrow to the innocent children (the tune to "On Wisconsin" that was used in the Pomato Soup advertisement actually kills Leon) is, on the whole, an undeniably beneficial institution. It feeds the hungry, provides jobs, and gives Mrs. Carillon the wealth that makes her search and very existence possible. Although she desired to see social justice and to help the underdog, Raskin, who was successful at the stock market, also always perceived the opportunities open to people who work hard.

In addition to work and the difficulties of material success, a second typically American motif in *The Mysterious Disappearance* is guilt. Although this will become most important in *the tattooed potato & other clues* and *Westing Game,* guilt is already a driving force in the lives of many Raskin characters in this novel. Tina feels guilty, for example, for having incited the riot in Bloomingdale's by yelling "fire," because it gets Mrs. Carillon put in jail. She cannot bring herself to explain the situation, but she feels terrible as Mrs. Carillon's legal difficulties deepen.

Feeling guilty, of course, is the prerogative only of the well-intentioned but weak character so familiar in much of American literature. Without the desire to do good, and the perception to understand what good is, mistaken and wrong actions make no impact on a character. Many people were responsible for the scarlet letter, but only Dimmesdale really paid the price. In *The Mysterious Disappearance,* the Fishes and Carillons are hustled to the hereafter before they can come to any assessment of what their greed has done, so they have no opportunity to court our sympathy, much less our approval. Pinky Newton is too obtuse and self-satisfied to see that his cowardice and bungling has nearly ruined a life. Only Mrs. Carillon and Leon have a chance to feel guilt and to try to make amends.

Mrs. Carillon, for example, unintentionally causes Tina and Tony, her adopted twins, to wish to return to the orphanage out of loneliness and rootlessness. Because of her own abuse-ridden upbringing, she has no idea how to bring up children. She thinks not hitting them might be enough. But when she sees that her search for Leon has been selfish in its single-mindedness, she promptly asks for another chance and becomes a better mother. In so innocent a character, knowing right and doing it are the same thing. Leon, whose disappearance causes such a radical change in Mrs. Carillon's life, is more complex. But he is not guilty of anything more malevolent than weakness and poor judgment in friends. Self-absorbed in his own miseries, he seeks only to escape from his memory of the soup business and the childhood marriage, but he sends someone else to talk to Mrs. Carillon. His kind letters and gift of the racehorse show the desire to do right despite his loveless childhood.

If we can see here that life can cause caring people to be the innocent cause of other people's misery, we also see, more strongly than in the other works, that a beneficent providence can translate the bad situations into good. Mrs. Carillon's bad education left her a much more interesting and lovable person than a good education would have. Her unselfish decision to slow the search in favor of the children actually speeds the search. Her devotion to Leon saves her for her marriage to Augie. Her "wasted" life, properly viewed, gives her everything she wants. Although Raskin's work is characterized by happy endings, this happy ending is much more optimistic than the endings of her other novels.

Mysteries and Perception

The problem of perception, a major theme in the Raskin picture books, is expanded and further developed in her novels, or "puzzle mysteries." Raskin implied that her choice of a mystery format was without special significance. "I don't read mysteries. I like reading true crime, and I have a true crime section on my bookshelves. But I do think kids like mystery, and it certainly keeps the plot moving" (Conmire, 179). But the mystery story is central to both her themes and her style.

Mystery readers, for example, seem to thrive on formula mysteries because the mystery is always solved in a tidy, comprehensible manner. Unlike life, one can count on fictional mysteries working out; thus, they fill a psychological need. Raskin's heroines seem to benefit from something like this phenomenon. Mrs. Carillon gains freedom and emotional maturity from her search. When the mystery is painfully solved, she emerges shaken but free. Working out a mystery, even when the case does not seem to have to do directly with the actual problem, has this effect in Raskin novels.

Mysteries also distance the reader from the emotional reality of crime. As Bunter says in Dorothy Sayers's *Busman's Honeymoon,* "her ladyship's pen has so adorned the subject as to render the body of a murdered millionaire as agreeable to the contemplative mind as is that of a ripe burgundy to the discriminating palate."[2] The mystery leads one to think of a corpse as a problem to be solved rather than a tragedy that shakes one's faith or a sight that sears one's sensibilities. Raskin desired this distance from directly discussing emotional issues and shows this, as well, in her choice of a humorous style, the classic human defense against tragedy.

It is a peculiarity of Raskin novels that early reviews used such words as "madcap" to describe them and implied that nothing but nonsense was to be found between the covers. Although Ellen Raskin, is, indeed, funny and highly original, she wrote black humor. Those who failed to see that Mrs. Carillon is an abused child and that the novel is about the tragic effects of an unhappy childhood missed the subject matter in part because of the distancing presentation. Perhaps it is hard to believe in the children's plight when it is described so flamboyantly and melodramatically and when the heroine's picture looks as though she has a black caterpillar sitting on top of her head. It is also possible, of course, that the emotional content of the novels would not have been missed if the novels had been written for the adult market where this kind of humor is more expected. James Marshall, a picture-book humorist of rare quality, told Stephen Harrigan he has similar trouble with reviewers calling him "zany."[3]

Finally, as Eric A. Kimmel pointed out, mysteries are exercises in perception, the subject that Raskin returned to over and over (Kimmel, 639). The good mystery, as everyone knows, has perfectly fair clues presented in such a way that the reader does not perceive their significance at the time. When the pattern emerges, the clues can be properly seen. Raskin puzzle mysteries thus reinforce their theme in their form. The Raskin heroine must see the clues in a particular way to solve the mystery; she must see life in a particular way to achieve her true identity.

Mrs. Carillon is unlike her later heroines (Mona Newton, Dickory Dock, and the Westing heirs) in that she has unusually clear perception from the first. This is because, unlike the others, she does not care or know what other people are likely to think. She is innocent of convention and does not have to change in order to see things properly.

Mrs. Carillon's innocence in this regard can be seen in the underwear episode on the night of the first duck dinner with Augie Kunkel. Tina suggests that perhaps Mrs. Carillon would like lacy underwear for Mother's Day, since her friend's mother always wears lacy underwear in case she is in a traffic accident. Mrs. Carillon agrees that this is a concern of many women: "I often think of that myself; that's why I never wear any underwear at all" (74). She doesn't understand the shocked reaction to this simple statement: the twins and Augie are embarrassed and flabbergasted. It emerges that Mrs. Carillon's plan for being hit by a truck has nothing to do with immodesty; she always wears a bathing suit like the one she had on the last time Leon saw her, so if she should be hit, the newspapers will print "Unidentified Woman in Purple Flowered Swimsuit Hit by Truck," and Leon will remember and find her. She is too single-minded and primitive to have acquired any social taboos.

Mrs. Carillon's freedom from inhibition is generally responsible for the happiness of her life. She never considers taking advice from anyone who ought to advise her, she never reacts to other people's ill temper, and she never allows other people's worries to prevent her from making friends. The hippies, the women in the House of Detention, and the twins all come usefully into her life because it never occurs to her to question their stories or their life-styles. She occasionally appears to be helping the undeserving, but to her the undeserving are more interesting, anyway.

Mrs. Carillon's perception, then, is accurate. The novel appears to recommend her way of seeing things, with special note of her social and racial egalitarianism. Although the steady, analytic methods and careful verification of Augie and the twins is the correct method of naming the missing and decoding the message, Mrs. Carillon's instincts lead the way.

Mrs. Carillon is right in thinking that the child is father of the man in Leon's case. He remains interested in horses, and so does Pinky. The novel finally shows that the conventional view that dictated that her search was foolish and that Leon must be dead or he would have asked for money is false. Leon does not care about money (particularly soup money), and he is found. Mrs. Carillon's unconventional search thus is both successful and personally rewarding.

Naming

Ellen Raskin's novels are concerned with naming as a corollary to her concern with perception and truth. A name, after all, can change the way that people see one, and the importance of one's actual given name to one's identity is a problem with varying answers. Its arbitrary nature, for example, is puzzling. "Leon" and "Noel," in *The Mysterious Disappearance* are the same four letters reversed, but they point to very different social, ethnic, and religious backgrounds. "Christmas Bells" and "Noel Carillon" mean the same thing, but one is a "genteel" name for a man, and one is the name for a seasonal phenomenon, which, by custom, might also be an adjective/noun name of the kind often given to racehorses. "Remus," as Mona tried to tell her family in *Figgs & phantoms,* has one set of associations when it is part of "Uncle Remus" and another when it is part of a set with "Romulus."

When a name is so changeable by its nature, it is hard to understand why the person who has it cannot change it, but this is so. A true name apparently stands for the truth about the thing it names, however whimsical the original namer may have been. Augie Kunkel's ability as a namer is, therefore, central to *The Mysterious Disappearance,* a story about false identities, but it is difficult to see which naming attribute makes him best qualified for the job, and what naming, exactly, entails. For example, one of Augie's favorable attributes appears to be "keeping to facts not opinions." When Tina asks Augie what one would call a set of one boy/one girl Siamese twins, Augie doesn't argue that there cannot be any or chide her about lying at school, he calls it "a medical phenomenon."

This appears to be a combination of three separate processes in one. First, Augie is making a name for something that does not exist, but naming it seems to make the imagined thing real. Naming gives substance to that which is without physical reality, which has some importance in Raskin's vision, particularly in regard to imagining other worlds, happy endings, and heavens. Second, "medical phenomenon" also shows that Augie knows something about Siamese twins, though, so the name has evolved from the heart of the matter; naming is a proof of knowing about something, not an empty accomplishment. One can see that this would be the case, too, with Augie's tour of Mrs. Carillon's livingroom. He notices a *"Blanc de Chine* triple lichee box," and a "Regency carved giltwood *fauteuil."* The correct name, in such cases, demonstrates expertise. Tony does not ask, "How do you know what they're called?" He asks, "How do you know all that?" (72). Mrs. Carillon had never known what they were, of course, so her choice of such rare objects is another evidence of her sound judgment based on her ignorance of convention.

Finally, the act of naming in this novel appears to be an act of appreciation and acceptance. When Mrs. Carillon asks Augie to say grace at Thanksgiving, he recites the names of the dishes in

French. Mrs. Carillon's continued use of the Carillon name (which Augie endorses) shows acceptance of her life. She is demonstrably better able to handle her life than Leon, who tries to make his name sound more genteel and also lives under a pseudonym. His failure to confront his wife and his inability to confront his name are two parts of the same problem.

Happy Endings

The puzzle mystery ends, as mysteries promise that they will, with human justice and tidiness. *The Mysterious Disappearance of Leon (I Mean Noel)* is resolved with mercy for everyone but the blown-up parents, a few mean classmates, and mean Miss Oglethorpe. Yet Raskin's desire for a happy ending does not blind her to her concession to herself, her readers, and her format. "Most of the people in our story lived to a ripe old age. Some achieved fame; others love. One was hit by a truck and another disappeared; but when all is tallied and compared to real life, this is truly a happy ending" (146).

5

Figgs & phantoms

Each must find his own Capri.[1]

"Moaning Mona" was the hero with whom Raskin most clearly identified, and *Figgs & phantoms* was her favorite novel. The book concerns Mona Newton's attempt to reach her favorite relative (modeled on Raskin's step-Grandfather Hersh) after he dies, leaving her in a slough of adolescent misery and loneliness. Many children's stories explore the plight of a young person in this kind of sad situation; none has used the topic as Raskin does. *Figgs* is her funniest work; yet in this work she is most ingenuous about pain and sorrow.

Superficially, the quests of Mona and Mrs. Carillon (the heroine of *The Mysterious Disappearance*) are similar. Both characters are looking for a missing person, and both achieve a kind of insight or emotional reward through their search. But the heroines themselves are different. Mrs. Carillon was already irremediably unusual when she began her search, the product of an eccentric and selfish upbringing. Mona is still a child at home, cowed and made self-conscious by her own version of her town's conventional and narrow-minded disapproval of her mother's flamboyant family. Although Mrs. Carillon's point of view might be taken as a model, Mona's vision must be changed before she can become the person she ought to be.

Jacket illustration from *Figgs & phantoms* by Ellen Raskin. Text and illustrations © 1974 by Ellen Raskin. Reproduced by permission of the publisher, E. P. Dutton, a division of Penguin Books USA, Inc. Reproduced from original illustration in the Kerlan Collection, University of Minnesota.

Figgs & phantoms, like *The Mysterious Disappearance,* has a surprising and attractive appearance. Raskin separated this novel into six sections, each with four labeled subsections. This book's text is often decorated with exotic vaudeville playbills and beautiful curlicue signs with hilarious mistakes in them, produced by Mona's Uncle Truman, the Human Pretzel. It also contains letters about the Figgs's family heaven, newspaper announcements, and many pieces of verse from Milton, Blake, Schubert, and Gilbert and Sullivan operettas. As Constance Hieatt first noted, comments that Mona thinks the town of Pineapple is making about her family are set in italics, identified by a star in the text.[2] Real events are reported upon in italics with five stars above and below them. Section headings start with enormous ampersands and double rows of stars. In other words, the text is interesting and decorative. Because Raskin edited for appearance, her pages have style as well as surprises.

The first page of each new section is a full-page illustration. These are a kind of composite portrait indicating something about the heroine's state of mind. Some are of the pirate king, Miguel de Caprichos, who owns the island to which Uncle Flo escapes. Most, though, have Mona's face within a fig (her mother's family name) or pineapple (her town's name) with strangler fig vines and palm trees that represent, respectively, her fears and the literary island to which she goes to find her uncle. Mona's face starts shadowed and miserable and brightens in the final drawing, in which she looks out a window surrounded by the suddenly flowering vines. Mona's mental health, then, can be summarized in these naturalistic, though fantastic, drawings.

Figgs & phantoms is a novel about the role of books in creating the imagination. Mona lives a life involved with books but never reads them. Her Uncle Florence Italy Figg, a dealer in rare books with color plates, allows her to help run his business. She also asks for reference help from the town librarian, Miss Quigley. But the book jackets and the books' retail value, not contents, are what interests her, to her uncle's great regret.

Mona's love for her uncle combines with her financial ability in an innocent deception that she bullies him into practicing once a month. On that day, Ebenezer Bargain, a second-hand book dealer, puts his new purchases on the shelves and moves a few more volumes up to the very top shelf—higher than Mona and her very short uncle can reach—where he plans to save them for a retirement investment. Since Ebenezer is already 93, Mona has convinced her uncle to help her move a few of those rare volumes that might interest their own customers down to an accessible shelf where Uncle Flo can purchase them later. In order to reach them, Mona and her uncle dress up as the Figg-Newton Giant (Mona balances on his shoulders and wears a long costume) and parade through the town on the way to the bookstore. Once there, Mona stealthily describes the new top shelf books to her tiny uncle down below and moves down a few volumes at his direction. Giant Day, because it represents a tangible proof of their partnership, is a special event to Mona which she jealously guards from family encroachment. But it also represents a thematically significant gap in Mona's knowledge of her uncle's life: Ebenezer Bargain and Uncle Flo are best friends, and this tricky maneuver is well-known between them. Mona wants to be everything to her beloved uncle, but she does not (cannot) know even elementary facts about his daily life, much less his extensive and fantastic dream life.

Though the Figg-Newton Giant is imaginary and immortal, the partners are not. Uncle Flo, still worrying that he must leave Mona behind without the comfort he has always found in books, dies. Mona, inconsolable and jealously guarding her inconsolability, attempts to find him. Figgs, when they die, go to Capri. Since "each must find his own Capri" and her uncle was so fond of books, Mona reasons that his Capri is somewhere in his private library.

Her initial explorations of Joseph Conrad (her uncle's favorite author) are not reassuring. But, harrowed by Conrad's declaration that "we live, as we dream, alone"[3] and shattered by unintentionally hurting her favorite (black) librarian's feelings while trying to check out Conrad's sea novel *(The Nigger of the Narcissus)*, Mona hurtles herself into a coma and, simultaneously, to the shore of Uncle Flo's Capri. Her apprenticeship there under the direction of the Spanish author and would-be pirate Miguel de Caprichos enriches her perception of life and the role of the imagination.

Crowds

The family portrayed in *Figgs & phantoms* is fantastic and hilarious. Mona, the only Figg besides Uncle Flo to be likely to recognize that it is peculiar to have an Uncle Remus (his twin brother's name was Romulus) and that her grandparents spelled the famous showman Florenz Ziegfeld's name wrong when they named their son, shares her family's talents but not its bumbling incompetence. In a family in which her cousin Fido has been adopted to replace a dead bull terrier and is fed on Ken-L-Ration and her Uncle Remus's tour groups get lost in uncharted jungles and wastes, Mona is a self-conscious elitist who prefers the refinement of her Uncle Flo's taste in music and literature. Flo had to build this life-style himself after a 16-year career as "Dancing Baby Flo" and while enduring the personal tragedy of being pointed out as "almost a midget." The crowded world of Raskin picture books is here made literary fiction; exuberance is interesting, but it heightens the loneliness of the family member who does not fit in.

Uncle Flo and Mona share the world of Raskin's picture books, *Franklin Stein* or *Ghost in the Four-Room Apartment,* to some degree. Although they are misfits in the family, nonetheless they live in a personal, interested world in which there is no danger of their being ignored. But although he is loved, Uncle Flo is not understood; and, dearly loved, Mona cannot make her family understand. Loving each other, they dream alone. Raskin's insistence that this was a personal novel and her wealth of anecdotes about her mother's family ("the funny ones") shows us that a childhood spent in an extended relationship was fundamental in creating her world view. The parents' portraits here, as Sister Figg and Newt, are apparently not caricatures, nor portraits that would immediately strike others, but a creative enhancement of

certain characteristics remembered from her childhood. The
lively Raskinian family world is the source of both the entertainment possibilities of life and its fundamental tragedy.

Allusions

Sweet Fruits

Raskin had a wonderful time with the Figgs and figs. It is peculiar but true that the whole novel appears to have been conceived
as a kind of parlor game played with the "fig" entry in an encyclopedia, in spite of its personal nature. There was a fig tree growing over the wolf den where Romulus and Remus, the legendary
Roman founders, were brought up. Kadota, for whom Mona's vet-
erinary uncle is named, is a kind of fig. Uncle Truman's (the human pretzel) talent seems to refer to the fact that one of the
members of the fig tree family is the rubber tree (Ficus elastica)
and Florence's ambiguous name is a reference to the fact that
among the kinds of fig flowers is the pseudohermaphrodite, a
point that Raskin appeared to be enlarging on a little in her discussion of Phoebe on Capri. The vines that run around the picture
of Mona on the opening pages of each section, are "stranglers,"
the roots of a kind of fig tree that starts its life as a seed left in
the top of another tree (a palm, for example) by an animal and
then sends down roots, encircling and possibly killing the parent
plant by their profusion, until they reach the ground below.

The·fig fertilization cycle is just as Raskin describes in the book
when she has the family diary explain how Figgs complete their
existence by returning to "capri." This "capri" is not the Italian
island (though this enters the picture, too), but rather a place that
somehow metaphorically resembles the caprifig tree. In the fig
fruit's growth cycle, the desirable, sweet fig is fertilized by wasps
that must hatch from wild caprifig trees because the caprifig has
female flowers in which they can lay eggs. As the new wasps
emerge from the caprifigs, they are dusted with the tree's male
pollen. If branches from the caprifig tree are placed in the fig

trees before the insects emerge, the emerging wasps then enter the female flowers of the fig tree, pollinating the crop as they do so. This helps the people who want to eat the figs. However, since the sweet fig flowers are the wrong shape for laying eggs, if the helpful insects are to complete their own life cycle, they then must find a real caprifig tree with the short-styled flowers they are seeking. The process of putting the caprifig branches in the desirable fig trees is called "caprification."

Both the "strangler" vines and the exotic, ancient caprification process lend themselves to poetic metaphors about the Figg family, about Mona's dilemma, and about the completion process that the believing Figgs are seeking in Capri. However, because of their hardiness and their location in ancient countries, fig trees were already associated with many religious customs before Raskin added her Pineapple Figgs to the roster.

The fig was sacred to Bacchus, and both Bacchus and Romulus were (sometimes) vegetative gods who died and then revived in the spring.[4] Figs are mentioned frequently in the Bible. The prophet Amos, for example, was a fig dresser, a person who cuts open figs on the Sycomore fig (Ficus sycomorus) to render them edible when mature. The Bo tree (Ficus religiosa) is regarded as sacred by both Brahmans and Buddhists. In other words, there is a diverse spiritual heritage associated with members of the fig family.

Making a novel about moody adolescence and death out of figs is something like the process Raskin sees in poetry *(Paper Zoo):* a combination of freedom and structure. The figs offered the challenge of a kind of game in which ingredients are given and have to be used in a rational way by the players. The puzzle mystery structure does something like the same thing. It did not make the novels easier to write, as it might for a formula writer; Raskin indicates, for example, that it wasn't until a late draft of *Westing Game* that it was clear that Westing wasn't dead. She did not know how the story was going to come out. The structure, rather, seems to be the discipline that gave the books order, whereas the fancy was what made them individual.

Blake, Milton, and Conrad's *Lord Jim*

The literary allusions in *Figgs & phantoms* are to books in Raskin's own collection of rare books and to one imaginary book, *Las
Hanzañas Fantásticas,* the adventures of the would-be pirate,
Miguel de Caprichos, who is greeted with the Pirate King's song,
"It is, it is, a glorious thing, to be a Pirate King!" from *The Pirates
of Penzance* when he enters company. Caprichos is his island, and
it is after Uncle Florence finds this amazing imaginary island and
fellow dreamer in the Bargain Book Store that he knows where
to spend eternity and feels free to leave for his Capri.

The rest of the books—even *Wonderful Characters,* a book of
humans with strange deformities—are real books. The most important in *Figgs & phantoms* are by Milton, Blake, and Conrad.
Milton and particularly Blake were favorites of Raskin and seem
to be here because both had highly developed imaginations and
the ability to create convincing otherworldly places like the one
to which Uncle Flo has escaped. The quotation "Frowning, frowning night," which Mona hears on Capri, comes from Blake's *Songs
of Innocence,* for which Raskin composed music and illustrations.[5]
In her address at Simmons College, "Me and Blake, Blake and
Me," she said that among the many qualities she shared with
Blake was "an acceptance of wonders" (350). She understood how
Blake could entertain biblical prophets in his home, she said, because as a girl she had entertained a might-have-been Elijah,
herself.

> My great-grandmother lived in Sheboygan, Wiscon-
> sin . . . and my family—my mother, father, sister,
> grandmother, grandfather—and I went to my great-
> grandmother's house for Passover. Now, my great-grand-
> mother was one of the very few Jews who lived in
> Sheboygan, a small town with maybe two or three
> Jewish families. The time was the Depression, and every
> tramp knew about Jewish houses on Passover night.
> During the Passover ceremony there is one point at
> which one of the men leaves the table and opens the door
> to let in God's messenger, who is going to announce the

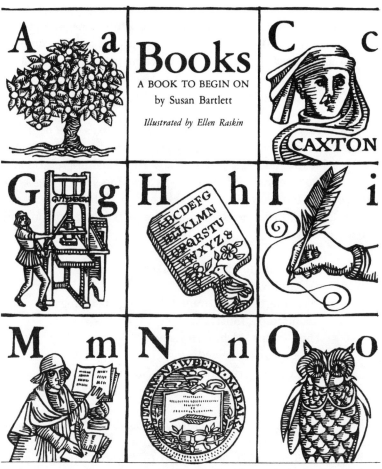

Illustration from front cover of *Books: A Book to Begin On* by Susan Bartlett.
© 1986 by Susan Bartlett. Illustrations © 1968 by Ellen Raskin. Reproduced
by permission of Henry Holt & Company, Inc. Original artwork from the Kerlan
Collection, University of Minnesota.

Messiah. At our Passovers every time a tramp would
come in and sit down at the place set for the prophet at
the table. Well, as a child, who was I to say he was not
Elijah? I certainly wouldn't have expected him to come
in a business suit, you know; he came in poverty. So it's
an image that has stayed with me all my life—accepting
the wondrous, just as Blake did. (350)

Susan Metcalfe, Raskin's daughter, emphasizes the degree to
which her mother was a rational person, given to discussing ideas
at the table, not feelings. But she says that Raskin's relationship
to Blake was intense. When she was working with *Songs of Innocence,* she felt he was right in the room with her.

The Pirate's threat in *Figgs & phantoms* is taken from Milton's
Paradise Lost:

> Where all life dies, death lives,
>   and Nature breeds,
> Perverse, all monstrous, all prodigious things.
> Abominable, inutterable, and worse
> Than fables yet have feigned,
>   or fear conceived,
> Gorgons and Hydras, and Chimeras dire.
>
>   (*Figgs,* 113)

Like Blake's prophetic works *Paradise Lost* describes out-of-earth
locations with conviction and power. Here, Milton's grand, ponderous description of Hell is evoked to frighten Mona from her
uninvited intrusion into Uncle Flo's afterlife. Mona, a nonreader,
has no majestic worlds to choose from. Uncle Flo had many and
wanted her to have many, too. To Uncle Flo, it is unacceptable to
live without imaginative resources, and his best ones are those
that others have invented for him. "From books I built my dream;
in a book I found Capri" (84).

In *Figgs & phantoms,* the books most often mentioned are the
novels of Conrad. Uncle Flo loves them, Mona pretends to have
an interest in collecting them, and Fido researches them for her.

Conrad appears to be introduced to show not only the rich possibilities of human existence, but also the practical necessity for
Florence's elaborate escapes. Florence Figg loved *Heart of Darkness;* he undoubtedly appreciated its accuracy. But if he believed
that vision of human depravity, it could only have reaffirmed his
intention to provide himself with an alternative to his own flawed
daily living. The Conrad stories are, then, thematically significant to *Figgs & phantoms,* but they are even more important
technically.

"I don't, even if I could do it, want my characters to grow and
develop and change" ("Materials"), Raskin has said. Instead, she
sought to show the reader a number of characters (some unlike-
able) who she then rounded out, filling in more and more information about them until the reader realizes that the first
impression was partial or misleading: "They're not the way they
seem." This technique is the most important of the many literary
echoes of Joseph Conrad in *Figgs & phantoms,* a technique most
obviously seen in Conrad's portrait of the court-martialed sailor
in *Lord Jim* or Kurtz in *Heart of Darkness.* Both men are thought
by many to be one kind of person and found later to be another.

The primary importance of the technique in *Figgs & phantoms*
lies in the heroine's perception of her family. As Constance Hieatt
points out, Mona has a faulty perception of the relationship between her family and the town: she feels that they are constantly
talked about and perceived as ridiculous (Hieatt, 133). She herself thinks they are ridiculous. Although this view is partial,
rather than wrong, one of the major strands of the book involves
Mona's coming to see her family as other people really see them.
They may, in fact, talk about the flamboyant Figgs, but they love
Sister Figg (the perpetual cheerleader, tap-dancer, and pageant
arranger) as much as the reader does, and everyone is proud and
happy to be in a Figg-instigated community celebration. It is true
that Mona's father, Newt Newton, loses money on every car that
comes in or out of his used car lot, but his good nature and weakness for flashy, unreliable automobiles make him loved rather
than scorned. Like Lord Jim, even Truman the Human Pretzel
has unusually developed heroic depths: He risked his own death

to bring Mona back from Uncle Flo's Capri. The Figgs don't change, but Mona's ability to perceive them does.

The rich literary allusions in *Figgs & phantoms* are appropriate in a book about book collecting and the pleasures of reading. They are also Raskin's own inspiration in the uses of the imagination.

Perception

In Capri, Miguel de Caprichos diagnoses Mona as self-centered and dreamless. Self-centeredness has kept her from being a loving child to her family, for example. While she was still a victim of faulty perception (she didn't want to hurt them), it didn't occur to her that she was hurting them because she never saw anything but her own misery. This is why the traumatic Miss Quigley incident is key to Mona's crisis and recovery. She sees in the library incident, finally, that it is possible to hurt someone cruelly without ever intending it. When Mona starts really looking at her mother and her Uncle Flo, she is able to be kind to both.

Mona's self-centeredness has also kept her from seeing the world around her. The island Uncle Flo has chosen for his Capri is an island where one can have any life one imagines. The Pirate, himself, engages in remarkable heroic sea battles; Uncle Flo has a wife, an infant daughter, a concert career in music, and Leonardo's *Mona Lisa*. But Mona cannot use the gift of creating-by-imagining on the island because she has never looked at anything but hamburgers and her old sofa well enough to make them real. She needs the long life that the Pirate and her family hope she will want to have in order to see the world properly. The pirate will not let her return to Capri when she dies if she has nothing to contribute. He will not let her strew his own literary home with tasteless objects and philistine wishes. She must, obviously, learn to see what is the best.

Dreamlessness, the second fault that the Pirate criticizes in Mona, is due to Mona's belief that pretending is childish. She frowns on childishness in any form because she is a teenager and because her parents are so clearly going to be children forever. But the inability to pretend leaves her defenseless in an imperfect world. She lives in misery because she cannot escape from death and from reality, and she does not desire to live in her current state. In Raskin's world, imagination is the appropriate and only way to live. As the Pirate tells Mona, "Your charming uncle and my dearest friend, Florence Figg . . . has married Phoebe twenty-six times since arriving in Caprichos." "In real life sweet moments are short and dulled by time" (123). *Figgs & phantoms* reaffirms what Raskin's early picture book contended: Iris Fogel's decision to take her spectacles off when she wants to is only sensible.

Uncle Florence was a wise man, an indulgent brother, and a good friend, despite being four foot six with fingers too short to play the piano and a body too small to invite the romance and domestic life he desired. With Mona's tastes and refinement, he cheerfully tapped out his "Dancing Baby Flo" act for his neighbors annually at his flamboyant sister's request. The secret of his contentment was his ability to borrow other people's dreams. He found his wife in Gilbert and Sullivan, his philosophy in Schubert, his neighbors in *Wonderful Characters,* his Capri in a book called *Las Hazañas Fantásticas.* If Mona learns to read books, as well as sell them, she too will be able to live long and learn. She will be able to make her own happiness, as all Raskin characters must.

Capri

It is books, finally, that alter the reality at the heart of Raskin's novel. Uncle Flo did live alone; Mona was cut off from his greater reality, his dream life, all the years that she hoped she was his dearest friend and his reason for living. Mona will still have to live alone. The child who returns from Capri will indulge her family because she doesn't wish to be unkind to them, but she shares her secrets with no one. She lies to her cousin Fido when he asks her about Uncle Flo; her real allies will always be people like Miss Quigley and her uncle, not her boisterous relations.

But the arguments that support this isolated and depressing state of being as the real truth are altered in the novel by the counterarguments about imagination. When Mona deserves to return to Capri, the Pirate will let her in. The people who want to find the would-be pirate's world are neighbors in the lonely crowd. The island of Caprichos has room for Mona's pink palm tree and all of Uncle Flo's guests. Further, it is a *book* that makes the Figg-Newton Giant real. Ebenezer Bargain's elegant printing of Mona's school composition about the Giant gives a beautiful form to the positive side of Mona's relationship with her uncle: they had loved each other very much.

Raskin's identification with Mona and fond remembrance of her step-grandfather may somewhat distort an equally interesting aspect of the novel. If Mona represents a part of Raskin's perception of her youth, Uncle Flo is surely a counterpart of her own middle age. The same age as Raskin (mid-forties) and also prematurely afflicted with a painful, arthritic condition, Uncle Flo's desire to leave for Capri but reluctance to leave his family appears to parallel the author's feelings. Although Raskin had creative outlets that Flo lacked, though she wrote when her hands could no longer work at the woodcuts and pointillism of her earlier illustrations, and though she played the stockmarket when she could no longer play the piano or harpsichord, *her* body, too, interfered with her ability to do the things she loved and to stay with people she loved.

Intentional, logical escapism hardly seems like escapism, especially when the creation of Capri is so bound up with Raskin's art. What seems to be a strong other-worldly streak also appears to be the thing least recognized in the woman herself. But her favorites (Blake and Milton and Velazquez) her many references to angels and artistic inspiration add up to a spiritual sensibility unusual in a woman so otherwise allied to the toughness and vitality of living. Her unswerving vision of the inadequacies of life always seems balanced by the belief that the individual should somehow have the ability to do something about it, to have control. When the physical controls fail, imagination is that control.

Though *The Westing Game* received the Newbery Prize and is undoubtedly a more approachable novel, *Figgs & phantoms* is Raskin's richest and best.

6

the tattooed potato & other clues

An artist must strive for beauty in all things, Ser-
geant, even in constabulary affairs.[1]

the tattooed potato & other clues, like *Figgs & phantoms,* seems
to speak to the most profound interests of Raskin's life through
the things closest to her. *Figgs* is about the role of books in life;
the tattooed potato is about art and life. Also, *the tattooed potato*
has thematic ties to *The Westing Game,* Raskin's last published
novel. While Mrs. Carillon and Mona are trying to find missing
people, Dickory Dock (the heroine of *the tattooed potato*) and the
Westing heirs are trying to find the secret identity of people who
want to be identified. Garson and Westing both give clues and
training to their apprentices in an effort to hand on their legacies
and to have a companion to share their burdens. Both use games
to train their heirs: Garson uses the detective cases and his one-
word identification game; Westing uses chess and the Westing
Game itself. Both are motivated in their activities by a desire to
undo wrong that they unintentionally committed, but for which
they feel intolerable guilt.

Dickory Dock, a first-year art student who is studying on a
scholarship and sharing her brother's walk-up railroad flat, is
hired by Garson, a well-to-do painter with a house in Greenwich
Village, to run errands, take care of his painting supplies, and

answer his door. This job, which broadens Dickory's experience of
painting, art, and affluence, also comes to include detective work.
Joseph Quinn, chief of detectives for the New York City Police,
falls into the habit of consulting Garson on detective cases. This
strange custom is justified on the grounds that Garson boasted
at a society party that the deceptions of a clever criminal could
only be seen through by a person with an artist's eye for truth.
Since Garson seems curiously reluctant to dismiss the Chief, he
and Dickory attempt to solve the cases, for which the chapters of
the book are named.

Dickory's qualification for her position at Garson's house is that
she is, as his advertisement specified, quiet, observant, and a native New Yorker. Native New Yorkers, it turns out, are suspicious
of everyone but not afraid to answer the door. In this novel, unlike
Figgs & phantoms, there is every reason for suspicion. Few people
in the novel but Dickory's friend George are who they claim to be
(even unassuming George has something like an assumed name).
Nearly everyone else is a criminal, a blackmail victim, a phony, a
murderer, or an undercover policeman. Even the innocent characters are linked by complex associations and patterns, and simple actions have reverberations that their perpetrators could
never have expected. *tattooed potato* has two mysteries at its
heart, which, when solved, lay to rest the incidents haunting the
major characters and show Dickory how to achieve beauty in this
sordid, yet colorful, world.

Dickory's tragedy is straightforward. Her parents, who ran a
pawn shop, were murdered just before Dickory graduated from
high school. The crime has never been solved. A beautiful antique
watch that played "Oranges and Lemons" was stolen at the time
of the murder. With some art books, the watch had been pawned
by a poor young artist and inspired Dickory's first interest in art.
Fortunately, she has a scholarship to attend art school, where she
is the best student in her class. But her home surroundings do
not support her efforts. Her brother and sister-in-law live miserable lives in a tenement; helpless themselves, they cannot further
her desire to find something better.

Garson's tragedy is much more mysterious. Although he is extravagantly successful and lives in a lovely house (Raskin used her own house in Greenwich Village for the model), his activities do not always seem to make much sense. Why would he rent a portion of his home to people who are clearly gangsters? Why does he have a picture framer, who is brain-damaged and frightening to look at, living in the basement? Why does he want Dickory to spend her time identifying the people who come to the door? Why does he own so many costumes? Why are there always messy painting taborets for Dickory to clean, when Garson uses different colors and cleans up after himself? Why is his entry in the painters' encyclopedia clearly invented?

Dickory's amusing and interesting job at Garson's is part odd jobs and part apprenticeship. From the job, she learns more about art materials and painting, and with the money in the generous salary she can actually buy some, which is useful to her own progress. As an apprentice, she learns how to solve mysteries, an activity Garson calls "seeing with an artist's eye for truth." Garson and Dickory practice seeing through disguises and disguising themselves. Dickory is being given the ideal training to find out the things that are so puzzling about her own employer, who is sometimes also her friend.

The design for this novel is simpler than that of the previous ones. Each section/case begins with a stylishly designed black page. Each section is further divided into brief chapters occasionally broken by reference entries, police descriptions, and verse.

Names: "I am Christina Rossetti"

Dickory and her brother, Donald, are both plagued by having the last name of "Dock." Strangers continually quote the nursery rhyme and the cartoon; this affliction has substantially altered their lives. But the other characters' names are also interesting. The minor characters Dinkel, Winkle, Hinkle, and Finkel are hilariously confusing. One of the criminals, like Uncle Flo, goes by the name of Francis, although she is a Frances. George, who is as embarrassed being "George Washington" as his family was when they changed their emigrant name to sound patriotic, has an uncle who is pretending to be two men named "Eldon Feodor Zyzyskczuk." Julius Panzpresser, the clothing manufacturer, Shrimps Marinara, and Manny Mallomar have Restoration comedy names that describe their essential features, as Garson's one-word identification game demonstrates. And "Rossetti," which means the shy Victorian poet, Christina, to Garson and Dickory, sounds like a Mafia gangster to the criminals and the Chief of Police.

Although intentionally assuming a new name may be useful under some circumstances (Garson and Dickory achieve a new relationship when they reverse their names and become the detectives Kod and Noserag), it is clear in this novel, as in the others, that no good would come of Dickory's denying her name or identity. Dickory is going to have to learn to live with her nursery rhyme name and the background that goes with it. By the end of the novel, "meritorious compassion" (acquired by guilt) and newly instilled self-worth have made her a person who can. But achieving a personal identity is not the only or the best goal in *the tattooed potato,* and accuracy is not the only goal in naming.

If truth was good, then naming something aright would be the highest good still. But the art world in *tattooed potato* looks at the truth about human nature, and the truth is ugly. "Vanity. Greed. Jealousy. Hatred" (69) Garson tells Dickory that what he can teach her is "How to see through frills and facades; how to see through disguises. How to see with an artist's eye" (24). If Dickory, who is an apt pupil, learns everything that Garson has to teach her along these lines, few of the things she sees in his own house will be very likeable. One of the things she will certainly see is that Garson is being blackmailed, for example, and so are all the other people who come to the door.

But artists also "strive for beauty in all things," and beauty in human affairs is compassion and love. The demands of beauty have to be met simultaneously with the demands of truth: This is why Garson is disguised.

When he tells Dickory that "No one deserves to stand naked and maskless before complete strangers, before the ogling world"

(135), Garson is explaining why he sacrificed his ability to be an important artist in his own time in order to protect the sensibilities and souls of the people he paints. He cannot stop painting, and he cannot stop seeing with an artist's eye; but he *can* prevent the paintings from revealing the truth about his sitters in their lifetimes. Thus, whenever he paints a portrait, he hides the masterpiece that tells the truth and gives the sitter the slick, flattering society portrait that will make him or her happy. His own public identity, therefore, is that of a shallow dabbler, when it could have been that of the premier painter of his times: his early work is heavily collected and celebrated.

Although Garson and the Police Chief both have reasons for their dark vision of humanity, and other people would not feel compelled to make this choice, it is evidently a moral one in the novel: a deliberate sacrifice of vanity and greed to compassion. Garson is willing to be a phony; under the circumstances, no greater sacrifice is possible. Although Dickory will have to learn to live with the name "Dickory Dock," "Garson" is a better name for her employer, in a moral sense, than his own name, Edgar Sonneborg.

Freaks: "The word for Isaac is 'deaf-mute'"

Raskin was interested in people who have to live with an exterior or a life that is publicly acknowledged to be unusual or freakish. Because she hid her own emotions from others, as well as her own illness, and because she was interested in the dichotomy between appearance and reality in all her books, we assume that the idea of not being able to keep differences hidden must have struck her as particularly cruel. She discussed freakishness in her picture book *The World's Greatest Freak Show,* as well as in *Figgs & phantoms.* Since Raskin (like Garson) was interested in physical appearances in order to paint them and obliged to omit no truthful wart from her own perception of others, the often-cited advice of looking only at the character or personality of other people could not be the whole solution to the problem of unusual appearances to Raskin. She needed to incorporate the real physical appearance into her moral perception.

In *the tattooed potato,* the unkindness of the crowd is a factor in explaining why a person, any person, should be able to stay private and unrevealed. "The ogling crowd" is one reason Garson cannot let his truthful portraits be seen. But a second reason is even more powerful: humans are vain and cannot accept the truth about themselves. They will suffer from knowing the truth even more than they will from hearing other people's views. Garson's roommate, for example, ran out in front of a truck when he perceived that Garson had painted him as an untalented clown.

"The artist's eye" does see what a person looks like: many of Garson's undisguisings have to do with spotting physical features that other people don't see: pear-shaped figure, no beard, tremble in hand, fat rolls on the neck. But these are features that call for no moral judgment. His portraits are "truthful" or "slick" depending on whether he captures the spirit and truth of the person's whole being. Although his masterpieces, at least the mature ones, are "suffused with compassion" (95), moral and spiritual defects, often hidden by money or well-groomed outward appearance, are the sources of his satire.

Therefore, Isaac Bickerstaffe, the deformed man who lives in Garson's basement, is not a "monster" because he is gentle and helpful. The right term for him is "deaf-mute" because he cannot hear or speak, or "brain-damaged" because he had a serious head injury. He is also a good frame-maker and a loyal friend. Cookie Panzpresser shows herself to be a perceptive woman when she refers to Bickerstaffe as "young man" instead of reacting negatively to his unexpected appearance at the door, and it is notable that she is just as truthful and perceptive about herself.

It is also true, however, that in his past life, Isaac was a vain and sentimental person with no accurate picture of his own limitations as an artist. Rather than admit that he would not be a great painter, he ran in front of a truck. Rather than generously admit that his best friend had the talent he lacked, he grew jealous and brooding. These are very human qualities, but they are not admirable. His moral and physical limitations are also part of the truth about him that cannot be ducked by the artist. Garson has decided, however, that low as his opinion of the majority of humanity (and himself) is, beauty requires compassion and kindness to others. He could respect people more were they not vain, but since they are, he consciously caters to their vanity as a higher kindness. He will indulge their weakness as an apology for seeing it so clearly.

Although Garson cannot help but see that Dickory is often rather unkempt (Dickory's truthful self-description would be "dirty hair," "ragged fingernails," "roundish face," "flattish nose"), his public assessment of her is "haunted," an intuitive insight into Dickory's melancholy state. By linking her hauntedness to a quality he sees in the angels painted by the Renaissance artist Piero della Francesca, he caters to her vanity almost as much as he does to that of his sitters, because Dickory has not yet had a chance to establish her character with him. But in Dickory's case, the boost it gives her self-esteem makes her into the person that Garson says she resembles. Piero della Francesca angels are not pretty, they are better: righteous, noble, and human. Dickory looks at them and decides she can rise above her environment, that she ought always to be truthful and not a phony, that she should stand for right even if she might profit from wrong. She is willing to sacrifice to be kind. Garson's other portraits do not make people noble. Garson's insight about Dickory develops her potential; her moral potential is clearly a more important quality than the condition of her hair, which results from poverty and hopelessness.

The problem of freakishness is, in fact, much like the problem of coming to know any other human being in a Raskin book. People are the sum of all their parts, not just one or two qualities. One does not stop with appearance, any more than one denies appearance. One puts the pieces together before making an assessment. It is the misfortune of people with a striking appearance to be summed up by the ogling crowd before they have a chance to establish themselves. This overemphasis on exteriors also can help people to produce a false impression to fool others, but the artist's eye can always see through it. The artist intuitively knows the real from the superficial. Dickory criticizes Garson's picture of the judge because it "said nothing about the lawyer, nothing about the artist. It was a slick and shallow illustration" (19). The artist's eye needs both accuracy *and* moral vision. Viewed under such circumstances, the "freak" will be dealt with more honestly in the studio of a real artist than anywhere else, for the artist must bring both perspective and judgment to the portrait.

Allusions: "My heart is like a singing bird"

Like *Figgs & phantoms, the tattooed potato* contains many references to other works, but they are usually explained more fully in the text than they were in the previous novel. Garson and Dickory have a great deal of fun pretending mysteries, with an atmosphere that is a mixture of Sherlock Holmes, the Policemen's Chorus from *The Pirates of Penzance,* and Humphrey Bogart as Sam Spade. As one might expect, Garson is more expansive and lighthearted when he is taking on another role. Although as amateurs and dilettantes of crime, Garson and Dickory do not have the uneasiness of the Policeman's Chorus ("When constabulary duty's to be done, to be done, the policeman's lot is not a happy one"), Garson does counsel Dickory that an artist must strive for beauty in all things, even in constabulary affairs.

The songs in *the tattooed potato* are the nursery rhyme, "Hickory, Dickory, Dock," which Joseph Quinn elaborates upon whenever he sees Dickory; the nursery rhyme attributed to the eighteenth-century Isaac Bickerstaffe; and the nursery tune "Oranges and Lemons" played by the antique watch that starts and ends the action of the novel.

"Hickory, Dickory, Dock" explains why Dickory's name is such a burden. The nursery game "Oranges and Lemons" has a haunting tune mimicking church bells that is appropriate to an enamelled antique watch but belied by the words. The words to the song ("'When will you pay me?' say the Bells of Old Bailey / 'When I am rich,' say the Bells of Shoreditch") are strangely mercenary and at odds with the melody, and the game ends in actual violence. Like "London Bridge," which the game resembles, the players forming the arch bring down their arms trapping the player going under and chant, "Here is the candle to light you to bed / Here is the chopper to chop off your head." The watch's connection with Dickory's parents' murder, Dickory's own near-murder, and, simultaneously, her own growing awareness of beauty, make it a good symbol of the relationship of art and life in the novel.

Similarly, the name "Isaac Bickerstaffe" seems to serve the same function of presenting a misleading or disguised truth. Garson's Isaac and at least two of the three eighteenth-century writers using the name Isaac Bickerstaffe were using pseudonyms. Garson says he gave the name to the monstrous man in his basement because the lines, "I care for nobody, no, not I, if nobody cares for me," from the song "There was a jolly miller once" popularized in an opera by one of the Bickerstaffes, seemed to him to describe the look on Isaac's mutilated face. For his own reasons, of course, Garson also needed a new name for his old friend, since Isaac was going to share in his own disappearance.

But Isaac's face, if it does bring the rhyme to mind, is simply another misleading outward appearance. As the novel tells us, Isaac is willing to risk his own life for the people he cares about: He is willing to do it for Dickory. And Garson, in particular, cares about Isaac very much. The truth about Isaac's life is as different from his rhyme as the words to "Oranges and Lemons" are from their tinkling antique tune.

The allusions in *Figgs & phantoms* were primarily to poets and musicians whose strong sense of other worlds helped prepare Uncle Flo to find one of his own. The most important allusions in *the tattooed potato* serve a similar function. Dickory does not want to leave Earth; she only wants to leave behind ugliness and brutality, and the vision of herself as a Piero della Francesca angel does this for her. The angels, she thinks, manage to be angelic even when they are immersed in human life. "Feet planted solidly on earth, their eyes stared dreamily upon unimaginable visions of heaven." (*tp*, 59) When Dickory imagines herself as a Piero della Francesca angel, she refuses to take the mobsters in the first floor apartment seriously.

"Hey, brat. No more asking my visitors' names, you
hear?" Mallomar yelled from his doorway. "Did you hear
me, you lousy snoop?"

She did not hear. The angel wafted up the stairs, ears
sealed to secular profanities. (60)

Although Dickory gets so carried away that Garson wonders if
she is on drugs, the vision is salutary. Without a vision of the
beautiful, it would not be possible to live uncorrupted with so
much seaminess and corruption around her. The desire for beauty
is the beginning of the ability to create it. Christina Rossetti's
poem "My heart is like a singing bird" similarly gives Dickory an
ideal of happy ecstasy to strive for in a life that has been singu-
larly bereft of happiness or beauty.

Garson and her art lessons show her the beautiful. Garson also
gives her the confidence necessary to try to achieve it. Her silly
name, her impoverished and depressing background, her murdered parents, her unkempt looks have all undermined Dickory's
hopefulness. Her struggle to complete assignments and achieve
decency in her brother and sister-in-law's flat is deadening. Their
lives are drudgery, their tastes are philistine, and her brother, in
his worse moments, is jealous of her chance to do something that
she enjoys.

Garson gives her the vision of herself as a Piero della Francesca
angel and gives her a beautiful self-image. He tells her to make
her name mean something the way Christina Rossetti's did and
gives her hope. He is kind and understanding, so she can give
kindness back to her family. She can also give a brighter vision
back to him.

Perception: "You were wrong about Cookie"

Although Garson is valuable in training his apprentice's ability
to perceive, Dickory eventually has something to contribute to his
own perception. Garson's vision, after all, has also been influ-

3. And so he was quiet, & that very night,
As Tom was a-sleeping, he had such a sight!
That thousands of sweepers, Dick, Joe, Ned & Jack,
Were all of them lock'd up in coffins of black.

Illustration from *Songs of Innocence* by William Blake. © 1966 by Ellen Raskin. Reproduced by permission of Doubleday, a division of Bantam, Doubleday, Dell Publishing Group, Inc. Artwork reproduced from original in the Kerlan Collection, University of Minnesota.

enced by his early experience. If a tragedy had not resulted from his friend's response to truth, he might have had more faith in human nature, in life, and in his own character. Dickory sees the banana heiress's portrait as "sordidness . . . somehow fused with compassion" (95). If Garson paints the truth, he, like Augie, also accepts it and understands it. He is not really a heartless murderer ruthlessly exposing his fellow men out of vanity as he is apt to think.

Further, his response to his fellow men (indulgence, phoniness) is not always necessary. Not only are some people able to take the truth, but some truths are not sordid. The "genteel lady" portrait of Cookie Panzpresser is neither her vain dream nor her husband's. The truth (flourishing, prancing, cheerily vulgar Cookie) was what her husband, Garson, and the reader saw and loved. Dickory can restore Garson's vision a little, since she respects his need for secrecy but has not had his tragic experience.

Finally, if life is a condition in which bad things happen that people never planned or hoped, but for which they are guilty, life also includes positive outcomes that were never intended. The Oranges and Lemons watch and art books, pawned by a struggling student, were the catalysts to start Dickory on her own life's work and to bring her to Garson's door. A world in which there is work, beauty, and kindness is not as bad a world as he fears.

Set in the house in which she was living, *the tattooed potato & other clues* is Susan Metcalfe's favorite of her mother's novels. Even without her familiarity with the well-realized house that forms the structure for the action, this seems a reasonable choice. Raskin writes here about the role of art and beauty in life, and, with reading, this was central to what was important to her. In this book, too, she brings her previous explorations of perception to a partial conclusion when she defines the role of the artist in perception, although *The Westing Game* continues the discussion of masks and disguises.

the tattooed potato is also an intermediate point in the exploration of guilt in Raskin novels. Garson is the most guilt-ridden of the Raskin characters, yet he demonstrates for others, if not for himself, that good can come out of bad, that guilt can be the mother of compassion. This optimistic note is not demonstrated so fully in *tattooed potato* as in *Westing Game,* yet its presence, as well as the greater accessibility of the allusions of art and literature, may make it appeal to a wider audience than *Figgs.*

Dickory's adventure is a wild contrast of urban brashness and color with the beauty found in art. Although Dickory needs the one to survive the other, the reader is entertained and instructed by both. Piero della Francesca's angels inspire by their humanity. Dickory is funny when she interprets that stance as aloofness; she is wiser when she sees that beauty in human affairs is kindness. Cookie Panzpresser is silly, but she too is worthy. *tattooed potato* both recognizes the appeal of escape through art and wades right into its inspiration: life.

7

The Westing Game

> The solution is simple if you know whom you are
> looking for.[1]

Of all the Raskin puzzle mysteries, *The Westing Game* (1979 winner of the Newbery Medal and Raskin's last published novel) is
most like a classic mystery story. Inspired by the Bicentennial
and Howard Hughes's will, *The Westing Game* involves 16 heirs,
residents in a strange apartment building on the shore of Lake
Michigan in Raskin's native Wisconsin, who seek to inherit the
estate of their "Uncle Sam," a local industrialist who has died
under sinister circumstances.

All Raskin books have many eccentric characters, but *The Westing Game* pairs all 16 in roles of major importance as they try to
solve the clues that will give them the Westing fortune. Raskin's
earlier technique of equating solving the mystery with solving the
personal and perceptual problems of the heroine is here multi-
plied by 8, since each pair of heirs—while ostensibly trying to
become millionaires—is really getting an unexpected chance to
live a fuller life.

The Westing Game is dense with clues, details, and hilarious
grotesquery. To an adult who thinks of mysteries as a quick es-
capist read, the text may seem difficult. More accurately, the text
favors the slow or unconventional reader, who pays attention to

the pauses on each page. The text is separated, not only into chapters (which are brief and do not start on new pages) but also by "bullets" (large round printing dots that divide the text on at least every other page). Because Raskin edited her manuscripts for appearance, each section of the novel starts and ends attractively, and the text is also often broken by lists, advertisements, and other material that is set off by indentation or by typeface. The child who comes to *The Westing Game* without preconceptions is apt to stop at the end of each section to summarize the clues and new details on the spot: thus, the text may seem more like a game than a novel. To someone who reads quickly, each rereading will add new details and understanding, since Raskin's clues are set out obviously but fiendishly disguised by the wealth of details and interesting character development.

As I have suggested in chapter 5, *The Westing Game* is the novel that most fully develops Raskin's theory that characters do not change, a theory that she mentioned when she gave *The Westing Game* materials to the Children's Book Center at the University of Wisconsin. Since her books depend heavily on "things are not what they seem"—that is, characters are often disguised and the novels and picture books contain many surprises about them—this belief must be central to an understanding of Raskin's work.

It is easiest to see how the "character who doesn't change" operates in a novel by looking at the plot of Conrad's *Lord Jim*. Joseph Conrad was a favorite author of Raskin's, who collected his rare editions just as Uncle Flo did in *Figgs & phantoms,* and he was influential in how she thought about life. *Lord Jim* is a novel about a young officer who makes the mistake of leaving many innocent passengers on a ship that he thinks is about to sink. He responds to the fatal word, "jump," which swings the balance, with other circumstances of the time and place, and ruins his career.

The *Lord Jim* example shows several important factors that bear upon *The Westing Game*. First, whether a character is a hero or a monster is partly a matter of environment and chance. As Conrad's Jim's whole life shows, he also could be heroically self-sacrificing, and the Jim that was broken at the court-martial trial was only one aspect of the man. Thus, since we necessarily have only partial views of each character (or person, for that matter) who comes before us, anyone may have the ability to seem different to us without changing.

Second, the Conrad example illustrates that no person is wholly one thing or the other: Each has the potential to be swayed by the moment and to do unpremeditated harm or good. Under these circumstances, it is especially important to decide on one's principles and act in accordance with them, if one wants to have any control over one's life. As Westing says in his will, "Life, too, is senseless unless you know who you are, what you want, and which way the wind blows" (39). The unformed, unexamined person is the one with the most to fear from chance.

Third, the *Lord Jim* model may indicate that moral or personal judgments should be made with tolerance and humility.

In the works of a novelist who wrote about unhappy families and alienated children, this point of view is important because of the freedom it can bring, as it does, for example, in the case of *Jane Eyre*. A Jane Eyre who goes to her grave blaming her Aunt Reed for her miserable life could not be the mature, independent heroine we see at the end of the novel. *The Westing Game* has a more comfortable ending than the other novels. This is due most significantly neither to the all-American theme nor to the extravagant number of satisfactory endings she generously distributes to all and sundry, but to her handling of Grace Windsor Wexler, mother of the heroines Angela and Turtle.

Since Raskin undoubtedly felt the resentment toward her own mother that we all feel in the novel toward Grace, this is the darkest portrait of her parents found in her writing. Raskin did identify herself as Angela and her sister as Turtle, and the unequal but equally destructive treatment of the siblings is the reason for the resentment and identification. Raskin was not writing history, however—her mother was no advocate of early marriage, for example—and one must remember that the qualities of Cookie and Sister Figg were also associated with her mother in Raskin's mind. Although this is a resentful portrayal, it is interesting that

Raskin's heroines can control their old painful feelings, as well as their fortunes, undoubtedly to a degree difficult to achieve in real life.

In previous Raskin books, there was no major character so personally repellent to its author (or reader) as Grace Wexler. She is a smothering mother to her beautiful daughter Angela while completely rejecting her homely daughter Turtle. A racist, she makes both the black judge (Judge Ford) and Chinese Mr. Hoo feel actively uncomfortable in her presence. She lives a perfectly useless, artificially well-groomed life as a social climber and name dropper, spending more money than her husband makes and pretending to be an interior decorator. Her conventional ideas extend to an iron control over her eldest daughter's life. She pressures Angela into giving up her own career plans in order to embroider trousseau linen for an early marriage to an eligible doctor.

Grace's view of her daughters and treatment of her daughters has the damaging potential that only family influence can have. Angela thinks she is only a pretty face, a person with no importance beyond her marriageability and nothing in common with the girls who used to be her college classmates. It is clear that she is potentially suicidal, like her cousin Violet, who died for a similar reason. But Grace never realizes that she has abused Angela, any more than she realizes that she has neglected Turtle. No more capable than the families in Raskin's other novels of understanding her children or perceiving the wrong she has done yet infinitely more destructive, Grace surely deserves to be rejected and punished.

But Raskin (who blew up Mrs. Carillon's parents and put Miss Oglethorpe in jail) does not do it here. *The Westing Game* approaches tiresome, destructive Gracie with a vision of conquering love. The novel not only fails to punish or merely tolerate this hateful mother; it appreciates her. It shows that she is a victim of the very conventions she seeks to urge upon her eldest daughter. It demonstrates that, given a second chance by the Westing Game, she can develop her own inherited talent as an astute businesswoman and live with affectionate good will toward her unusual family. Her children both achieve happiness—the neglected child wins love and the Westing fortune—and both are able to preserve their family ties. With this sympathetic understanding of a formidable parent, Raskin's novel and heroines achieve the mature forgiveness that alone can free the victims from an unhappy past.

"Eight Imperfect Pairs of Heirs"

"Eight Imperfect Pairs of Heirs" was Raskin's working title for *The Westing Game,* a title helpfully pointing to a pattern that may be missed in the elaborate search for clues. *The Westing Game* is a successful mystery, but the quality that won it the Newbery Medal is its combination of classic mystery with significant thematic material.

Westing Game, then, matches the 16 chosen heirs of Sam Westing into 8 partnerships: Denton Deere, Angela's internist fiance, with Chris Theodorakis, handicapped birdwatcher; Sydelle Pulaski, eccentric Polish secretary, with Angela Wexler; Theo Theodorakis, sensitive, resentful brother of Chris, with Doug Hoo, hearty jock; Judge Ford with Sandy the Doorman; Otis Amber, idiot deliveryman, with Crow, the cleaning woman and soup kitchen operator; Jake Wexler, podiatrist and bookie, with Madame Hoo, lonely immigrant; Gracie Wexler with Mr. Hoo, bitter inventor and unsuccessful restauranteur; and Turtle Wexler, shin-kicking financier, with Flora Baumbach, motherly dressmaker. Each heir has needs or flaws; each is helped by having a partner. Although the Westing Game makes only one person genuinely wealthy, each heir receives many advantages and a happy ending from playing the game. Thus, the value of interpersonal relationships is strongly urged and the possibility of succeeding in life through reaching out to others and helping one another along is illustrated. This was a hard lesson for the ingenious Westing, and it is also a characteristic Raskin perspective in a story about capitalism and greed.

Second Chances

In addition to the partnerships that are so productive, there are
a number of deeper relationships within *The Westing Game* that
explain why the will was written in the first place. Sam Westing
and his wife in many ways resemble the Wexler couple, just as
Angela Wexler resembles Violet Westing, their daughter. Both
mothers failed their children through being overly concerned with
social prestige and being insensitive to their children's real per-
sonalities and needs. Both fathers are well-intentioned but too
weak to affect their daughters' lives. Jake Wexler is very much
like the bumbling, lovable Newt Newton in *Figgs & phantoms*
(and like Raskin's own father), but here we see that being a weak
parent makes being lovable a very negligible virtue. This similar-
ity of aims and methods has produced a similar result: Angela, as
the story opens, is in a desperate situation: She feels she has no
identity, no control over her own life, no possibility of a future,
and no help. The example of Violet Westing's suicide and the intervention of the Westing partnership give Angela the push to
change things and stand up for herself instead of being a passive
victim. By gathering the people who touched Violet's life, the will
eliminates a ghostly replay of her tragic death. It also gives two
sets of parents a second chance to become better people.

As in *the tattooed potato,* and, to a lesser degree, all the other
Raskin novels, guilt is the mother of compassion. Without his
daughter's suicide, it is doubtful that Westing ever would have
found a good life for himself or desired to do anything so ambi-
tious for others. In real life, this phenomenon is fortunately well
known. Emerson talked about it in the parable of the banyan tree
of the forest: that is, sometimes people who significantly benefit
society do so after their own lives have been interrupted by tragedy. Parents who lose their children to drugs or car accidents or
crime or illness, for example, are sometimes able to turn their
love outward to benefit others with similar problems. Their social
action, done in remembrance of the lost family member, benefits
society at large. Without the personal tragedy, no larger social
good would have been undertaken. Raskin is not so optimistic

elsewhere, but one can see that it is an extension of her desire to have control over life events.

Since Violet was so passive, her suicide caused guilt in her father, along with anger at her mother and her real boyfriend. Westing's reappearance as a philanthropist comes after he has forgiven those with whom he was angry (which he proves by including them, in some guise, in the Westing Game) and has also come to think that he might win love for himself, find a new heir, and repair some of the wrong he has done. The comforting feel of the novel comes from this optimism. Despite the uncompromising portrayal of tragic potential, the novel demonstrates a solid belief in the ability of human beings to improve their circumstances by their own efforts and to profit by a second chance.

Like most people, Westing had failures outside of his family circle as well. Some of the Westing heirs also represent these relationships. For example, Judge Ford and Mr. Hoo actually knew him in the past and had reason to regret the acquaintance. Mr. Hoo blames Westing for stealing his invention (the paper diaper) and Judge Ford blames him for putting her under an intolerable obligation. J. J. Ford, the daughter of one of his servants, was early recognized by Westing as a bright and deserving child and given special attention and a fine education. But his mentorship soured early because of Judge Ford's sensitivity to racial differences and because she could not trust Westing not to attempt to abuse their relationship by asking for favorable judgments. Although she never could have become the important person that she is without his help, Judge Ford's motivation in the game is to save whatever person Westing may be trying to hurt or destroy with his ingenious nonsense; she clearly feels that he is malicious and hurtful.

Because Raskin focuses a significant portion of the story through the judge's mind, we know her weaknesses as well as her strengths. Westing is no saint, but we can be sure that his intentions in her case were primarily good: Westing saw her potential; he wanted a chess-playing companion who might be trained for future corporate leadership. The damage done to the judge by the relationship is real and crippling, but, like the damage to his daughter, was done unintentionally. The Westing Game gives him a chance to undo that damage and to create another relationship with the judge. Because he, himself, trained her at chess, Westing also needs to be especially careful that the Judge does not succeed in overturning his plans.

Finally, the purpose of the Westing Game is to find an heir. This is what the Westing will is ostensibly about, of course, but the heirs do not know what the inheritance means. By making the will the kind of game that it is, Westing is hoping to find someone else with the skills to run Westing Products and, as important, to know his secrets. Like Garson in *the tattooed potato,* who trained his apprentice to become the only person who could see the man behind his vacuous mask, Westing waits at the center of his own labyrinth for another kindred spirit.

"We live as we dream, alone"—the Joseph Conrad quotation that so frightened Mona in *Figgs and phantoms*—can be modified partially if we share a love for something outside ourselves. In the Raskin books, these things are Raskin's own loves: literature, music, art, games of skill, and finance. In *Westing Game,* Westing's loves are finance and chess.

Allusions: The Son of Immigrants

The allusions in *Westing Game* are less specialized than in some of Raskin's other books, which perhaps explains the book's wider popular appeal. Mr. Westing, we find from the important newspaper obituary, was particularly fond of elaborate Fourth of July celebrations that allowed him to act in patriotic plays, dress in patriotic costumes, and set off elaborate fireworks. The Westing corpse is dressed as Uncle Sam, and disguises are important to Westing's strategy in the novel.

Westing was also a gamesman. He uses chess as a training method for skills and strategy. People who love chess are likely to be like Westing: fond of games, risks, winning. Dennis Flanagan called his wife "an assassin at the evening chessboard" (Flanagan, 395); she was also a highly successful investor in the stock market. Turtle, whose initial visit to the spooky Westing mansion was an attempt to raise the money for a subscription to the *Wall Street Journal,* shares her uncle's and her author's gamesmanship. She leads her willing but mystified partner through the heart-stopping risks and heady triumphs of trying to win the Westing Game through increasing her financial holdings. Turtle believes that "Buy Westing Paper Products" (a slogan in the will) means that she should invest in the stock. Her partner buys lots of paper towels.

The simultaneous occurrences of the American Bicentennial in 1976 and the dispute over the will of the reclusive and legendary billionaire Howard Hughes were the immediate inspirations for this novel: patriotism and capitalism. The heirs represent many of the immigrant populations that make up American society and represent, similarly, a cross section of social and economic classes. Chris Theodorakis, who is frequently misunderstood or underestimated because he suffers from a degenerative disease, also contributes to the inclusiveness of Raskin's cast.

The all-American cast not only echoes the melting pot nature of our society but also gives Raskin a chance to mention some of its problems. Judge Ford's insecurity despite her deserved prosperity and status could be and has been echoed by every member of society who exceeds expectations and must live with people who might be construed as hostile to her success. Mrs. Hoo, as a young immigrant with little knowledge of the English language, is characteristically exploited and isolated by her dependence. Indeed, Mrs. Hoo is so little able to communicate in the novel that she is the least successful character and seems as child-like and naive as her small stature, prettiness, and simple vocabulary would make her seem to the casual observer. Her later business career is not surprising but is necessarily limited in this novel.

In "Characters and Other Clues," Raskin tells us that Chris Theodorakis was based on a real young man (624). She mentions that she and her husband, while trying to entertain the boy and his father, were rejected from several New York City restaurants that refused to serve someone with his handicap. Theo and Angela cringe throughout the novel as people either assume the bright child is retarded and talk to him in an artificially simple voice or look away as he approaches. The novel tells us what we should know: Chris is a person. Though he does not solve the Westing Game, Chris comes closest to judging Westing's motivations, giving the real winner an important clue.

There are other references to illness and death throughout the novel that, given our knowledge that Raskin was ill and committed suicide several years later, acquire a melancholy significance. Sydelle, for example, invents a mysterious illness to attract attention, adopting a stiff-upper-lip stance as the most dramatic. "But pity me not, I shall live out my remaining time enjoying each precious day to the full" (27). Jake Wexler ineffectually prods away at people's painful feet; Sandy the doorman, according to Turtle's address to the jury, was a "dying man who chose his time to die" (171). Though Raskin is celebrating America in the novel, she is realistic about the kind of success America has had in living by its ideals and, as always, about the difficulties of living in any society.

"Uncle Sam," the name by which Westing is known in the will and in whose costume he is dressed in his coffin, bases his clues on a well-known patriotic song. His house is full of Fourth of July fireworks, which other characters borrow for incendiary purposes and which bring the Westing Game to a climax when the game is over. His will provides the would-be heirs with the same opportunity that he himself found in the "land of opportunity." Through intelligence, risk-taking, and hard work—and the sacrifice of his family and some moral perceptions—he became a great industrialist. Although Raskin sympathized with the labor movement (her own grandfather was a Wobbly), she had proved in her own life that hard work and intelligence could bring opportunities. Although she laughed at her "paean to capitalism," the child who was horribly frightened by the Great Depression did achieve the American dream. As we might expect, though, she paid a price.

Happy Endings

The Westing Game ends with a lavish distribution of desirable outcomes. No Westing heir is turned away. Although Raskin was giving herself a gift, as she said (Roginski, 172), by creating happy endings for the characters she had come to care about, the endings are as extravagant as the problems that preceded them. *The Westing Game* is black comedy, although it talks about real-life problems. The celebratory endings encourage us to believe that solutions to some problems may be worked out, but they do not take away the troubling nature of guilt, of family relationships, of racism, of disease, of loneliness. The ending, if anything, may even emphasize the extent to which the novel provides happiness that is unlikely in real life.

But the happy ending deserves a second look. What do the happy heirs receive? What makes them happy? A few heirs, such as the judge, Sydelle, and Crow, have problems that require special solutions. The judge needs to be free from the debt to Westing and to have the pleasure and pride of being a giver, not a receiver. In a novel about greed and making money, she is obsessed with freedom from obligation and completely indifferent to material goods. She is happy to hand over large checks to her partner; she welcomes the opportunity to help Chris Theodorakis with his academic career. Therefore, she is allowed to pay back her education, with interest, and continue her career with increased self-confidence. If her life seems a little solitary, except for the relationship with Chris, this is a reasonable outcome for a hard-working woman who finds it hard to trust and hard to be dependent.

Sydelle, the mistaken heir, wanted someone to think she was important; she gains a reputation for legendary wealth and marriage with her longtime employer, Mr. Schultz of Schultz Sausages. But before she marries and, while still playing the game, she gains a friend: Angela thought she was important first.

The most puzzling Westing heir is Crow, whom the judge feared was going to be victimized by Westing for being the immediate cause of his daughter's death. Crow is, in the language of the chess game, the sacrificed queen that Westing used to distract the heirs from his real object, the heir whose prize was to confess to her own identity. In a story in which "It's who you really are that counts," Angela was not the only person who had to name herself. Crow needs to accept who she is—the former faulty Mrs. Westing—and to feel the relief from some part of her guilt that confession brings. Painful as the moment is to the other heirs, who refuse to turn her in as an answer to the Westing Game for their own profit, the confession frees her from enough of her old life to start a new one. As the new wife of Otis Amber, she has support and love while pursuing her vocation: nurturing alcoholic street people as penance for having failed as a mother. Westing wanted her to have that chance, so he arranged that match.

These heirs already had satisfying jobs. Their needs were personal and needed personal solutions. But the rest of the heirs receive jobs that they can love as their happy endings. Remaining American to the end, *The Westing Game* keeps its essentially early American emphasis. It is not the riches, finally, that bring happiness: it is the work that is important.

Raskin's optimism, then, is based on personal experience and tough realism. She recognizes that it is easy to get lost in the flamboyant ugliness of everyday experience and to act in ways one never intended or visualized. But she offers a peculiarly American hope: if you can find satisfying work to do, it is possible to make happiness and to create beauty in our interesting but complex world.

8

Perspective

Raskin's original and unusual qualities set her apart from any other children's writer of her generation; her influence has allowed greater latitude and more sophisticated style within her genres. But the answer to a young person seeking more work like Ellen Raskin's is "There is no one else like Ellen Raskin." In a country of humor-loving, unpretentious people, we have as a nation contributed largely to earnest works for the young. Sid Fleischman said this during Raskin's lifetime,[1] and it remains true to a great extent. Though, as he noted, we have an elegant group of humorous writers for the nursery, junior novels do not adequately represent the comic response to life.

Of course, there are humorous books in which characters (often parents or teachers or siblings) are represented as bumbling or peculiar. This kind of book abounds, although often in not very distinguished forms. Raskin's canon represents, rather, the truly absurd, the universe in which the answers are not available in daily life, in which the human response to the awfulness of death is often to joke about it, and in which it cannot be denied that "we live as we dream, alone" in many ways. She was also strongly satiric about individual human and social weakness, a rarity in American children's literature since Wiggin and Twain at the turn of the century.

The impulse to meet misfortune with humor is so common in real life that its rarity in children's literature suggests a form of censorship, of hypocrisy, or simply narrowness of perspective. Raskin's hilarity represents in heightened and original form the plucky response to real problems. The courage and defiance that we understand lies at the root of humor in her books is necessary in a world to which we cannot be perfectly reconciled. In Raskin's books, as in Lewis Carroll's, absurdity is countered by heroines who win their games, although not without walking a thin line between managing and death. These heroines take their cues from a structure that will discipline their moves and provide a shape for their lives. In Raskin's contemporary American settings, gamesmanship is as important as it is in Wonderland or through the looking-glass.

Although life is often painful, it is never boring in a Raskin book. From her first picture book through *Westing Game,* Raskin's world is crowded with incident and eclectic characterization. There are monsters in the attic, the downstairs apartment, and the kitchen cupboards, and none of them has anything in common with the others beyond their difficulty in fitting into a human social sphere. There are pickles on the telephone, in a song from *Yeoman of the Guard,* in *Silly Songs and Sad,* and in those same kitchen cupboards; and each serving combines the silliness of the name and food with poignant human meaning. The world has had its share of symbolic roses. Raskin gave us symbolic pickles, and, given the nature of human reality, her symbolism makes a good deal of sense.

The Raskin minor characters often have a vividness and grotesque innocence that make a comparison with Dickens quite reasonable. Noel Carillon, Cookie and Julius Panzpresser, Truman Figg, and Rebecca Quigley have interesting possibilities that the reader sees, even when the major characters do not. Their interesting possibilities, too, are the logical extension of their adaptations to life. Persona peculiarities are treated tolerantly in Raskin's vision, in contrast to their portrayals in those books in which families and teachers are perceived with teenage rigidity. When life's complexity is admitted, a sensible person is not apt to sneer at someone else's successful adaptation. Tap dancing in cornflakes (or studying taps for morse code messages) can seem very gallant in the face of despair.

Raskin was a literary person, a great reader, and her works derive richness from allusions to the works of several other authors: Milton, Blake, James, Conrad, Rossetti, Gilbert. Although it might be said that drawing on artists unfamiliar to young people complicates Raskin's style, a work that uses the words of Milton to frighten or the works of Piero della Francesca to inspire is using both appropriately. Raskin's books are, among other things, about where to find beauty and how to use beauty to endure everyday life.

Raskin's style is efficient, demanding, and colloquial. It has the timing required by humor, but its beauty is visual, based on the appearance of the type, design, and illustrations. This unconventionality in the source of pleasure extends to the way that the readers themselves must assemble the two halves of a mystery (the solutions to the puzzle and the human solutions). The ability to do this is unrelated to the reader's age, but probably to freedom from preconceptions. To the reader who understands Raskin, it should be clear that *The Westing Game* and Dickens's *Christmas Carol* have similar things to say: the same awareness of human evil, the power of money to corrupt, the same reassuring belief in the possibility of a second chance. Both, indeed, rely as much on melodrama as on idealism. The one story's theme is explicit and its characters intentionally sentimental; the other's is implicit and the characters include a disgruntled inventor who recovers his spirits over the financial success of a paper insole called "Little Foot-eez." Paper insoles, like pickles, demand a different palette than plum pudding, although the two are not mutually exclusive.

These paper insoles inserted in a story about finding a second chance in life are typical of the bizarre and engrossing world in which the Raskin characters find themselves. The sincerity of the characters convinces us, not of this world's campiness (which also requires complete sincerity) but of its normalcy. Mrs. Carillon's daily change of purple bathing suits and Garson's potato tattoo have their own rationale. Raskin's radicalism comes from her own view of life and the view that she, with few companions, brought to her genre.

Raskin wrote as an outsider and from the position that both child and adult had equal importance, equal responsibility, and, finally, equal difficulty, in shaping their lives. Raskin's outsider status undoubtedly had to do partly with her childhood experience as a Jewish child in an alien culture. Her humor could certainly be compared to different aspects of "Jewish humor," the humor of a people with long, painful experience and practice at surviving it. But whatever the causes of an outsider sensibility and the costs of living with it, its assets for a writer are too well known to particularize. In her own books, this consciousness led Raskin to write about racial and social discrimination and discrimination against the handicapped with more honesty than is yet common 10 years after *The Westing Game* received the Newbery Award. She could not have done so had she not believed herself to be an outsider, despite her spectacular personal success and her comfortable life-style in later life. Further, since Raskin's experience as an outsider was tied to her childhood, the status of the child, too, is unusual in Raskin's books.

Two of Raskin's picture books, *Moe Q. McGlutch* and *Ghost in the Four-Room Apartment,* show the element of equality between characters that is seen in many Raskin books and is vital to their satiric content. These books are unusual in that all the characters are called by their first names, and the adult characters' status as fathers and mothers is not used to differentiate them from the children. All are responsible for their own activities, and none is privileged. Dumpling Fish's renaming as "Mrs. Carillon" at the age of five is the first of the name changes in *The Mysterious Disappearance* (a book about naming). This does the same thing that Raskin did in the picture books; it gives an independent life to a child who had been given grown-up problems along with her grown-up name. Unjust as the situation is, the name gives status and importance.

After *Mysterious Disappearance,* in which the parents are all blown up early, Raskin's novels are unusual in trying to consider the situations of both the adults and children, even when they may be each other's problem. This evenhandedness, and equal status, is indicated verbally by the fact that all the characters are known by their first names, as in the picture books. Raskin thus avoids the narcissism of the novel in which all the other family members are merely troublesome appendages to the hero's life, or the authoritarian stance in which the child's trouble is reduced in stature by being an attribute of immaturity. People are people in Raskin books, and she does not restrict the ability to live properly and think wisely to any one age group; nor are her sympathies limited to the child who might be the age of the typical reader.

Because Raskin distances us from the young person's difficulty by humor, she refuses for them the sentimentalizing that would inhibit their ability to survive and gives them the status due to people who can be mature and can cope. Their ability to extract amusement and enjoyment out of the situation is so many extra points. Their ability to be kind in an unkind world is shown to be an attribute of maturity.

Raskin said that readers who wrote to her came from many age ranges and degrees of ability. To some extent, they are the readers who like to work things out, from the toddlers who examine the pictures in *Spectacles* before they turn over the page, to the older readers who sort through the fair, but difficult, clues of the Westing Game. The readers of the novels, Raskin said, thought that "They were weird and I was weird and we were all weird together" (Hinchcliffe interview). She said that she got the readers she wanted. Her readers got what they wanted, too: books that are the solution to what to do about imperfect reality; books that contain wonders and visions of extravagant originality; books that laugh at evil while taking the plight of its victims seriously.

Notes and References

Chapter One

1. *the tattooed potato & other clues* (New York: Dutton, 1973), 135.
2. "The Creative Process of Ellen Raskin," videotape (Green Bay: University of Wisconsin, 1983); hereafter cited in text as "CP."
3. Alice Bach, "Ellen Raskin: Some Clues about Her Life," *Horn Book,* March–April 1985, 162–67; hereafter cited in text.
4. Dennis Flanagan, "The Raskin Conglomerate," *Horn Book,* August 1979, 392–95; hereafter cited in text.
5. "Characters and Other Clues," *Horn Book,* December 1978, 623; hereafter cited in text as "Characters."
6. "Newbery Medal Acceptance Speech," *Horn Book,* August 1979, 387; hereafter cited in text as "Newbery."
7. "An Interview with Ellen Raskin" by Dick Hinchcliffe, WHA Radio, Madison, Wisconsin, May 1979; hereafter cited in the text.
8. Lila Fink, telephone interviews and correspondence with the author, November 1989, January and September 1990; hereafter cited in the text.
9. "Banta Award Acceptance Speech," Milwaukee, Wisconsin, Midwest Federated Library Association Conference, 2 November 1979; hereafter cited in text as "Banta."
10. "Me and Blake, Blake and Me," in *Innocence and Experience,* ed. Barbara Harrison and Gregory Maguire (New York: Lothrop, Lee & Shepard, 1987), 347–53; hereafter cited in text as "Me and Blake."
11. Jim Roginski, "An Interview with Ellen Raskin," in *Behind the Covers: Interviews with Authors and Illustrators of Books for Children and Young Adults* (Littleton, Colo.: Libraries Unlimited, 1985), 170, 171; hereafter cited in text.
12. Susan Metcalfe, interview with author, August 1988; hereafter cited in text.
13. *"The Westing Game:* Explanation of the Manuscript Materials," Speech of 2 May 1978, audiotape at the Cooperative Children's Book Center, University of Wisconsin, Madison; hereafter cited in text as "Materials."
14. Ann Durell, interview with author, New York City, July 1987; hereafter cited in text.

Chapter Two

1. Isaac Asimov, Review, *Horn Book,* June 1967, 366.

2. Harry Stubbs, "Views of Science Books," *Horn Book,* June 1968, 338.

3. Jennifer Waller, "Maurice Sendak and the Blakean Vision of Childhood," *Children's Literature* 6 (1977): 130.

4. Afterword to *A Paper Zoo,* ed. Renée Karol Weiss (New York: Macmillan, 1968); hereafter cited in text.

5. Edward Ardizzone, "Creation of a Picture Book," in *Only Connect,* ed. Sheila Egoff, G. T. Stubbs, and L. F. Ashley (Toronto: Oxford, 1969), 347.

6. Illustrator's note to *Come Along!* by Rebecca Caudill (New York: Holt, 1969); hereafter cited in the text.

7. Afterword to *Goblin Market* by Christina Rossetti (New York: Dutton, 1970); hereafter cited in text.

8. Jeanie Watson, "'Men Sell Not Such in any Town': Christina Rossetti's Goblin Fruit of Fairy Tale," *Children's Literature* 12 (1984): 69.

Chapter Three

1. "Ellen Raskin," in *Something about the Author,* vol. 38, ed. Anne Conmire (Detroit: Gale Research, 1985), 177; hereafter cited in text.

2. William Moebius, "Introduction to Picturebook Codes," *Word & Image,* April–June 1986, 141–58; hereafter cited in text.

3. Perry Nodelman, *Words about Pictures: The Narrative Art of Children's Picture Books* (Athens: University of Georgia Press, 1988), 239; hereafter cited in text.

4. Eric A. Kimmel, "Ellen Raskin," in *Twentieth-Century Children's Writers,* 2d ed., ed. D. L. Kirkpatrick (New York: St. Martin's Press, 1983), 639; hereafter cited in text.

5. Arnold Lobel, "A Good Picture Book Should . . . ," in *Celebrating Children's Books: Essays on Children's Literature in Honor of Zena Sutherland,* ed. Betsy Hearne and Marilyn Kaye (New York: Lothrop, Lee & Shepard, 1981), 75.

Chapter Four

1. *The Mysterious Disappearance of Leon (I Mean Noel)* (New York: Dutton, 1971), 21; hereafter cited in text.

2. Dorothy L. Sayers, *Busman's Honeymoon* (New York: Harper & Row, 1937; reprinted 1986), 54.

3. Stephen Harrigan, "Growing up With George and Martha," *Texas Monthly* 15, no. 12 (1987): 188.

Chapter Five

1. *Figgs & phantoms* (New York: Dutton, 1973), 61; hereafter cited in text.

2. Constance Hieatt, "The Mystery of *Figgs & phantoms*," *Children's Literature* 13 (1985): 133; hereafter cited in text.

3. Joseph Conrad, *Heart of Darkness* (1902), *Collected Works* 21 vols. (London: Dent, 1961), 5:82.

4. Sir James Frazer, *The Golden Bough,* ed. Theodore H. Gaster (New York: New American Library, 1959), 108, 406.

5. *Songs of Innocence* by William Blake, 2 vols. (Garden City, N.Y.: Doubleday, 1966).

Chapter Six

1. *the tattooed potato & other clues,* 37; hereafter cited in the text.

Chapter Seven

1. *The Westing Game* (New York: Dutton, 1978), 39; hereafter cited in text.

Chapter Eight

1. Sid Fleischman, "Laughter and Children's Literature," *Horn Book,* October 1976, 465.

Selected Bibliography

Primary Works

Picture Books

And It Rained. New York: Atheneum, 1969.
A & The; or, William T. C. Baumgarten Comes to Town. New York: Atheneum, 1970.
Franklin Stein. New York: Atheneum, 1971.
Ghost in a Four-Room Apartment. New York: Atheneum, 1969.
Moe Q. McGlutch, He Smoked Too Much. New York: Parents, 1973.
Moose, Goose, and Little Nobody. New York: Parents, 1974.
Nothing Ever Happens on My Block. New York: Atheneum, 1966.
Silly Songs and Sad. New York: Crowell, 1967.
Spectacles. New York: Atheneum, 1968.
Twenty-Two, Twenty-Three. New York: Atheneum, 1976.
Who, Said Sue, Said Whoo? New York: Atheneum, 1973.
The World's Greatest Freak Show. New York: Atheneum, 1971.

Illustrations

Books: A Book to Begin On by Susan Bartlett. New York: Holt, 1968.
A Child's Christmas in Wales by Dylan Thomas. New York: New Directions, 1959.
Circles and Curves by Arthur Razzell and Kenneth Watts. Garden City, N.Y.: Doubleday, 1968.
Come Along! by Rebecca Caudill. New York: Holt, 1969.
D. H. Lawrence: Poems Selected for Young People. Edited by William Cole. New York: Viking, 1967.
Ellen Grae by Vera and Bill Cleaver. Philadelphia: Lippincott, 1967.
Goblin Market by Christina Rossetti. New York: Dutton, 1970.
Happy Christmas: Tales for Boys and Girls. Edited by Claire H. Bishop. New York: Daye, 1956.

Inatuk's Friend by Suzanne Stark Morrow. Boston: Little, Brown, 1968.

The Jewish Sabbath by Molly Cone. New York: Crowell, 1966.

The King of Men by Olivia Coolidge. Boston: Houghton Mifflin, 1966.

Lady Ellen Grae by Vera and Bill Cleaver. Philadelphia: Lippincott, 1968.

Mama, I Wish I Was Snow; Child, You'd Be Very Cold by Ruth Krauss. New York: Atheneum, 1962.

A Paper Zoo. Edited by Renée Karol Weiss. New York: Macmillan, 1968.

Paths of Poetry. Edited by Louis Untermeyer. New York: Delacorte, 1966.

Piping Down the Valleys Wild. Edited by Nancy Larrick. New York: Delacorte, 1968.

Poems of Edgar Allan Poe. Edited by Dwight Macdonald. New York: Crowell, 1965.

The Poems of Robert Herrick. Edited by Winfield Townley Scott. New York: Crowell, 1967.

Probability: The Science of Chance by Arthur Razzell and Kenneth Watts. Garden City, N.Y.: Doubleday, 1964.

A Question of Accuracy by Arthur Razzell and Kenneth Watts. Garden City, N.Y.: Doubleday, 1964.

Shrieks at Midnight. Edited by Sara and John Brewton. New York: Crowell, 1969.

Songs of Innocence by William Blake. 2 vols. Garden City, N.Y.: Doubleday, 1966.

Symmetry by Arthur Razzell and Kenneth Watts. Garden City, N.Y.: Doubleday, 1968.

This Is 4: The Idea of a Number by Arthur Razzell and Kenneth Watts. Garden City, N.Y.: Doubleday, 1964.

Three and the Shape of Three by Arthur Razzell and Kenneth Watts. Garden City, N.Y.: Doubleday, 1969.

We Alcotts by Aileen Fisher and Olive Rabe. New York: Atheneum, 1968.

We Dickinsons by Aileen Fisher and Olive Rabe. New York: Atheneum, 1965.

Novels

Figgs & phantoms. New York: Dutton, 1974; Penguin Puffin, 1989.

The Mysterious Disappearance of Leon (I Mean Noel). New York: Dutton, 1971; Penguin Puffin, 1989.

the tattooed potato & other clues. New York: Dutton, 1975; Penguin Puffin, 1989.

The Westing Game. New York: Dutton, 1978; Avon, 1984.

Essays and Speeches

"Banta Award Acceptance Speech." Milwaukee, Midwest Federated Library Association Conference, 2 November 1979. Audiotape at Cooperative Children's Book Center, University of Wisconsin, Madison.

"Characters and Other Clues." *Horn Book,* December 1978, 623.

"Me and Blake, Blake and Me." In *Innocence and Experience,* edited by Barbara Harrison and Gregory Maguire, 347–53. New York: Lothrop, Lee & Shepard, 1987.

"Newbery Medal Acceptance." *Horn Book,* August 1979, 390.

"Pictures: Where, Why, When . . . and How." Workshop at the Fine Art of Book Illustration Conference, May 1979, Madison, WI. Audiotape at University of Wisconsin, Madison.

"*The Westing Game:* Explanation of the Manuscript Materials." Speech of 2 May 1978. Audiotape at Cooperative Children's Book Center, University of Wisconsin, Madison.

"Writing from Wisconsin." Telephone interview on WHA Radio, October 1981. Audiotape at Cooperative Children's Book Center, University of Wisconsin, Madison.

Secondary Works

Bach, Alice. "Ellen Raskin: Some Clues about Her Life." *Horn Book,* April 1985, 162. Friend and colleague of Raskin reveals details of Raskin's illness after her death.

Conmire, Anne, ed. "Ellen Raskin." In *Something about the Author,* vol. 38, 172–81. Detroit: Gale Research, 1985. Quotations from Raskin's essays and illustrations from her books.

"The Creative Process of Ellen Raskin." Videotape (40 minutes). Green Bay: Wisconsin, Educational Television Network, 1983. Available from University of Wisconsin. Raskin discusses her early life against the background of Milwaukee, her work in her studio; children and professionals discuss her books and creative process.

Durell, Ann. Interview with author in New York City, July 1987; telephone response fall 1989.

Fink, Lila. Telephone interviews and correspondence with author November 1989; correspondence January 1990; telephone September 1990.

Flanagan, Dennis. Interview with author in New York City, July 1987. Correspondence 1987–89.

————. "The Raskin Conglomerate." *Horn Book,* August 1979, 394. Raskin's husband, editor of *Scientific American,* discusses Raskin's originality and versatility on the occasion of her Newbery Medal.

Hieatt, Constance. "The Mystery of *Figgs & phantoms.*" *Children's Literature* 13 (1985): 133. Excellent pioneering article on *Figgs.*

Hinchcliffe, Dick. "An Interview with Ellen Raskin." WHA Radio, Madison, Wisconsin, May 1979. Audiotape at University of Wisconsin Cooperative Children's Book Center, Madison. Interesting discussion of Wisconsin childhood and why Raskin left.

Kimmel, Eric A. "Ellen Raskin." In *Twentieth Century Children's Writers,* 639. 2d ed. New York: St. Martin's Press, 1983. Brief, but perceptive, entry.

Kruse, Ginny Moore. "A Whole New World and Beyond: The Ideas of Ellen Raskin Become Books." September 1979. Videotape at University of Wisconsin Cooperative Children's Book Center, Madison. Ginny Moore Kruse, director of Cooperative Children's Book Center at the University of Wisconsin and friend of Raskin, discusses Raskin's work.

Kruse, Ginny Moore, and Petkus, Monika. Interview on WHA Radio's "Morning People" on the occasion of Raskin's winning the Newbery Award, 12 January 1979. Videotape at University of Wisconsin Cooperative Children's Book Center, Madison. Brief interview.

Metcalfe, Susan. Interview with author in Far Hills, New Jersey, July 1988.

Roginski, Jim. "Interview with Ellen Raskin." In *Behind the Covers: Interviews with Authors and Illustrators of Books for Children and Young Adults,* 170, 171. Littleton, Colo.: Libraries Unlimited, 1985. Intelligent interview on life and work.

Index

The Author

Educated at Michigan State University (B.A., 1969) and Duke University (M.A., 1970; Ph.D., 1975), Marilynn Strasser Olson teaches in the English Department at Southwest Texas State University, San Marcos, Texas.

The Editor

Ruth K. MacDonald is a professor of English and head of the Department of English and Philosophy at Purdue University. She received her B.A. and M.A. in English from the University of Connecticut, her Ph.D. in English from Rutgers University, and her M.B.A. from the University of Texas at El Paso. To Twayne's United States and English Authors series she has contributed the volumes on Louisa May Alcott, Beatrix Potter, and Dr. Seuss. She is the author of *Literature for Children in England and America, 1646–1774* (1982).

ACG8075

6/6/91
S.O.

PS
3568
A696
Z8
1991

0 00 02 0513141 0
MIDDLEBURY COLLEGE